"I simply cannot say enough about Ortlund's treatment of the book of Proverbs. There is depth here—scholarship disguised as pastoral advice. There is breadth here—quoting diverse people from Descartes to Sherlock Holmes. There is heart here—the heart of an evangelist, a pastor, a friend, and one who truly understands the Word. *Proverbs: Wisdom That Works* shines God's light on your day in every area of life."

Woodrow Kroll, President, Back to the Bible; author, *Proverbs: God's Guide for Life's Choices*

"Ortlund not only speaks wisdom, he models how to speak it. He not only lights the way on how to preach Proverbs, but on how to walk in wisdom— and he makes me want to do both! Almost immediately I had two reactions: 'Why am I not preaching Proverbs right now?' and 'Why am I not wiser by now?' Turn here not just to hear about wisdom, but also to taste it. You'll find the savor reverently worshipful, theologically rich, and relentlessly practical."

John Kitchen, Senior Pastor, Stow Alliance Fellowship, Stow, Ohio; author, *Proverbs: A Mentor Commentary*

"*Proverbs: Wisdom That Works* models powerful, profound, relevant expository preaching. The expositions are God-centered, Christ-centered, practical, evangelistic, life-changing, and life-giving. For Proverbs 1–9, each exposition digs deeply into the meaning of the passage in its original context, connects it with the New Testament (especially with Jesus Christ), and demonstrates astutely its contemporary relevance with illustrations and quotations. The last seven chapters bring together various proverbs under seven topics: the tongue, humility, family, emotions, friendship, money, and life and death. The oral style provides easy reading for deep, wise insights. A superb source for preachers preparing a series of Christian sermons on the book of Proverbs and for Bible study groups interested in studying biblical wisdom."

Sidney Greidanus, Professor of Preaching Emeritus, Calvin Theological Seminary; author, *Preaching Christ from the Old Testament*

"The strength of Ray Ortlund's study of Proverbs is its Christ-centeredness. The wisdom of Proverbs loses none of its practical value, but rather is given its ultimate fulfillment as an expression of the wisdom of Christ."

Graeme Goldsworthy, Visiting Lecturer in Hermeneutics, Moore Theological College; author, *Preaching the Whole Bible as Christian Scripture*

"For the pastor who desires to preach Proverbs, this book will prove to be an important tool. Ortlund's scholarly giftedness and his pastoral passions combine to create an accurate, readable, and Christ-centered guide to Solomon's great book of 'love and faithfulness.'"

George W. Robertson, Senior Minister, The First Presbyterian Church, Augusta, Georgia; author, *Deuteronomy: More Grace, More Love*

"I have been an appreciative reader and user of R. Kent Hughes' series of Preaching the Word. It is therefore a joy to commend the most recent addition to that series in Ray Ortlund's *Proverbs: Wisdom That Works*. It goes without saying that we in the evangelical church have long needed an exposition of this book, for it really does deal with 'where the rubber meets the road' on the hard realities of living the Christian life. I enjoyed each chapter of Ray's exposition and with thanksgiving to our Lord commend this work to all of God's people—pastors, leaders, and laypersons. It touches on the basic fabric of life with a note of divine authority and practicality."

Walter C. Kaiser Jr., President Emeritus and Distinguished Professor of Old Testament and Ethics, Gordon-Conwell Theological Seminary

PROVERBS

PREACHING THE WORD
Edited by R. Kent Hughes

(((PREACHING *the* WORD)))

PROVERBS

WISDOM
That WORKS

RAY ORTLUND

R. Kent Hughes
Series Editor

WHEATON, ILLINOIS

Proverbs

Copyright © 2012 by Ray Ortlund

Published by Crossway
        1300 Crescent Street
        Wheaton, Illinois 60187

Cover design: Jon McGrath, Simplicated Studio

Cover image: Adam Greene, Illustrator

First printing 2012

Printed in the United States of America

Italics in Biblical quotes indicate emphasis added.

Unless otherwise indicated, Scripture quotations are from the ESV® Bible (The Holy Bible, English Standard Version®), copyright © 2001 by Crossway, a publishing ministry of Good News Publishers. Used by permission. All rights reserved.

Scripture references marked JB are from *The Jerusalem Bible*. Copyright © 1966, 1967, 1968 by Darton, Longman & Todd Ltd. and Doubleday & Co., Inc.

Scripture quotations marked KJV are from the *King James Version* of the Bible.

Scripture quotations marked NASB are from *The New American Standard Bible®*. Copyright © The Lockman Foundation 1960, 1962, 1963, 1968, 1971, 1972, 1973, 1975, 1977, 1995. Used by permission.

Scripture references marked NEB are from *The New English Bible* © The Delegates of the Oxford University Press and The Syndics of the Cambridge University Press, 1961, 1970.

Scripture references marked NIV are taken from The Holy Bible, New International Version®, NIV®. Copyright © 1973, 1978, 1984, 2011 by Biblica, Inc.™ Used by permission. All rights reserved worldwide.

Scripture references marked NKJV are from *The New King James Version*. Copyright © 1982, Thomas Nelson, Inc. Used by permission.

Scripture references marked NLT are from *The Holy Bible, New Living Translation*, copyright © 1996, 2004. Used by permission of Tyndale House Publishers, Inc., Wheaton, Ill., 60189. All rights reserved.

Scripture references marked NRSV are from *The New Revised Standard Version*. Copyright © 1989 by the Division of Christian Education of the National Council of the Churches of Christ in the U.S.A. Published by Thomas Nelson, Inc. Used by permission of the National Council of the Churches of Christ in the U.S.A.

Scripture references marked REB are from *The Revised English Bible*. Copyright © 1989, 2002 by Oxford University Press and Cambridge University Press. Published by Oxford University Press.

ISBN-13: 978-1-58134-883-5
ISBN-10: 1-58134-883-5
PDF ISBN: 978-1-4335-3104-0
Mobipocket ISBN: 978-1-4335-3105-7
ePub ISBN: 978-1-4335-3106-4

Library of Congress Cataloging-in-Publication Data

Ortlund, Ray
  Proverbs : wisdom that works / Ray Ortlund
    p. cm. (Preaching the Word)
  Includes bibliographical references and indexes.
  ISBN 978-1-58134-883-5 (hc)
  1. Bible. O.T. Proverbs—Commentaries. I. Title. II. Series.
BS1465.53.O78   2012
223'.7077—dc23   2011020710

Crossway is a publishing ministry of Good News Publishers.

VP		32	31	30	29	28	27	26	25	24	23
21	20	19	18	17	16	15	14	13	12	11	10

To Dr. Bruce K. Waltke
learned mentor, beloved friend

Contents

A Word to Those Who Preach the Word

There are times when I am preaching that I have especially sensed the pleasure of God. I usually become aware of it through the unnatural silence. The ever-present coughing ceases, and the pews stop creaking, bringing an almost physical quiet to the sanctuary—through which my words sail like arrows. I experience a heightened eloquence, so that the cadence and volume of my voice intensify the truth I am preaching.

There is nothing quite like it—the Holy Spirit filling one's sails, the sense of his pleasure, and the awareness that something is happening among one's hearers. This experience is, of course, not unique, for thousands of preachers have similar experiences, even greater ones.

What has happened when this takes place? How do we account for this sense of his smile? The answer for me has come from the ancient rhetorical categories of *logos*, *ethos*, and *pathos*.

The first reason for his smile is the *logos*—in terms of preaching, God's Word. This means that as we stand before God's people to proclaim his Word, we have done our homework. We have exegeted the passage, mined the significance of its words in their context, and applied sound hermeneutical principles in interpreting the text so that we understand what its words meant to its hearers. And it means that we have labored long until we can express in a sentence what the theme of the text is—so that our outline springs from the text. Then our preparation will be such that as we preach, we will not be preaching our own thoughts about God's Word, but God's actual Word, his *logos*. This is fundamental to pleasing him in preaching.

The second element in knowing God's smile in preaching is *ethos*—what you are as a person. There is a danger endemic to preaching, which is having your hands and heart cauterized by holy things. Phillips Brooks illustrated it by the analogy of a train conductor who comes to believe that he has been to the places he announces because of his long and loud heralding of them. And that is why Brooks insisted that preaching must be "the bringing of truth through personality." Though we can never perfectly embody the truth we preach, we must be subject to it, long for it, and make it as much a part of our ethos as possible. As the Puritan William Ames said, "Next to the Scriptures, nothing makes a sermon more to pierce, than when it comes out of the inward affection of the heart without any affectation." When a preacher's *ethos* backs up his *logos*, there will be the pleasure of God.

Last, there is *pathos*—personal passion and conviction. David Hume, the Scottish philosopher and skeptic, was once challenged as he was seen going to hear George Whitefield preach: "I thought you do not believe in the gospel." Hume replied, "I don't, but he does." Just so! When a preacher believes what he preaches, there will be passion. And this belief and requisite passion will know the smile of God.

The pleasure of God is a matter of *logos* (the Word), *ethos* (what you are), and *pathos* (your passion). As you preach the Word may you experience his smile—the Holy Spirit in your sails!

R. Kent Hughes

Preface

"Wisdom cries aloud in the street, in the markets she raises her voice" (Proverbs 1:20). The Wisdom of God does not stand aloof, as if she were too good for us. She graciously moves toward us, into our real world where we live and struggle day by day. She offers us her very best, if we will only listen. With the overwhelming flood of information and opinion in our times, much of it a mixture of spin, sound bites, and trivialities, it is a relief to turn back to the Bible. It is a relief to slow down and pay close attention to deep insights that have stood the test of time.

As we come to the book of Proverbs, God does not intend to crush us with layer upon layer of demand. He intends to *help* us. The book of Proverbs is practical help from God for weak people like us stumbling through daily life. It is his counsel for the perplexed, his strength for the defeated, his warning to the proud, his mercy for the broken. The book of Proverbs is the gospel—good news for the inept through the wisdom of Another. We have every reason to receive it with a whole heart.

Thank you for picking up this book. May God use it to bless you as you study the wisdom of his ancient sages. The book of Proverbs is one of the "many ways" God has spoken to us (Hebrews 1:1). It leads us to Christ. If you look for him here, you will find him.

I am happy to acknowledge a special debt of gratitude to the commentaries of Bruce Waltke, John Kitchen, and Derek Kidner. In addition, I was helped by the preaching of Tim Keller on Proverbs. The influence of these outstanding scholars and pastors is pervasive throughout this book.

I thank Dr. Kent Hughes for the privilege of contributing this Proverbs volume to his Preaching the Word series. I thank the wonderful people of Immanuel Church, Nashville, for sharing in my eagerness to grow in the wisdom of Christ.

It gratifies me deeply to dedicate this book to Dr. Waltke. From 1971 to 1975 he was my esteemed Old Testament professor in seminary. His professional training and personal influence marked me for life. I feel a debt of love great beyond any possibility of repayment.

Ray Ortlund
Immanuel Church
Nashville, Tennessee

1

Why the Book of Proverbs Matters

"Whoever is simple, let him turn in here!"

PROVERBS 9:4, 16

EVERYONE IS ON A PATH. Everyone is going somewhere. When we feel stuck, even when we feel trapped, the truth is, we are still in motion. Life is a journey, and the end of it all is not just a place but also a condition. We are *becoming* the end of our journey, wise or foolish, and every moment takes us closer there.

God cares about that. "For God so loved the world, that he gave his only Son, that whoever believes in him should not perish but have eternal life" (John 3:16). The Bible is the voice of God inviting us into his eternal life. During the Old Testament era God standardized his speaking to us in three ways. The priests taught his law, the prophets declared his word, and the sages or wise men gave his counsel (Jeremiah 18:18). Both the commands of the Law and the thunderings of the prophets spread out before us the gigantic truths of God, the metanarrative that makes sense of everything. But we need more. We live day by day in a world where "there are details of character small enough to escape the mesh of the law and the broadsides of the prophets, and yet decisive in personal dealings."[1] So God gave us more than the Law and the prophets. He also gave us wise counsel.

For example, Proverbs 27:14 in the NLT says, "A loud and cheerful greeting early in the morning will be taken as a curse!" We don't find that in the Ten Commandments or in Isaiah or Jeremiah. But a well-intentioned but

15

ill-timed greeting can backfire, and that's worth knowing! God thinks so. He cares about our understanding of the massive truths of our existence. But he also cares about the nuances that make a difference in our relationships and experiences every day. Even if we do seek the holiness of the Law, and we do, even if we are inspired by the visions of the prophets, and we are, we can still make a mess of our lives, our families, our churches, our workplaces, our communities if we are unwise. We need God's help moment by moment, down at the level where there are no hard and fast rules to go by. What kind of woman or man should I marry? Which career path should I take? How can I endure this suffering I can't escape? How should I spend my money? Through the book of Proverbs, God coaches us in the *wisdom* we need throughout the long and complicated path of our everyday lives.

It's the practicality of the book of Proverbs that some people underestimate. This book is indeed practical, but it is not simplistic or moralistic. What God is going after through this book is change deep inside our hearts. His wisdom sinks in as we mull over these Biblical proverbs slowly and thoughtfully. We need multiple exposures over time. This book is not a quick fix. It is ancient wisdom from long human experience endorsed by God himself. If we'll pay close attention, God will graciously make us into profound people.

The book of Proverbs is a gospel book, because it is part of the Bible. That means the book of Proverbs is good news for bad people. It is about grace for sinners. It is about hope for failures. It is about wisdom for idiots. This book is Jesus himself coming to us as our counselor, as our sage, as our life coach. The Lord Jesus Christ is a competent thinker for all times and all cultures. He is a genius. And he freely offers us, even us, his unique wisdom. Do you remember how he concluded his Sermon on the Mount? He defined the gospel as a call to wisdom: "Everyone then who hears these words of mine and does them will be *like a wise man* who built his house on the rock. . . . And everyone who hears these words of mine and does not do them will be *like a foolish man* who built his house on the sand" (Matthew 7:24, 26). Jesus is our priest and our prophet, but in the book of Proverbs we encounter Jesus as our mentor. Do you see him that way? You can have him that way—the universe's greatest expert on you. He alone is qualified to have that kind of say in your life.

Let's not patronize Jesus Christ as a nice man who gives us warm religious fuzzies while we turn to the "experts" (whoever they are), the seriously qualified people, for the challenges of real life. Jesus Christ is the shrewdest man who ever lived. No one ever outthought him. No one ever surprised him or cornered him in debate. He was always out ahead of everyone, both his friends and his enemies. Jesus Christ is the best counselor for all people in all seasons of life. The Old Testament prophesied that the Messiah would be anointed with the Spirit of wisdom and understanding, so that he would not judge by what his eyes see or decide disputes by what his ears hear (Isaiah 11:2, 3). In other words, our Messiah is not fooled by appearances or swayed by hearsay, like other leaders, even brilliant leaders. No one will ever pull the wool over his eyes. The Bible says that Jesus has eyes like a flame of fire, seeing through everything (Revelation 1:14). And God has given this super-smart expert to us as his best gift of amazing grace. The gospel says that Jesus *is* wisdom from God (1 Corinthians 1:30). It's why he surprises us. When he taught in his hometown synagogue, his neighbors were astonished and said, "Where did this man get this wisdom?" (Matthew 13:54). Solomon had been the wisest man in history. But when the Pharisees tested Jesus and he reminded them that the Queen of Sheba came from the ends of the earth to hear the wisdom of Solomon, she was so eager to learn, Jesus said to them, "Behold, something greater than Solomon is here" (Matthew 12:42). They didn't have to travel any distance. Wisdom incarnate was standing right there. But they were too sure of themselves to listen.

Let's not underrate what we have here in the book of Proverbs. Biblical wisdom is more than what we find in a fortune cookie. It is more than an optional add-on for people who want to upgrade their lives from, say, 4 to 7 on a scale of 1 to 10. This wisdom from Christ is a matter of life and death: "The teaching of the wise is a fountain of life, that one may turn away from the snares of death" (Proverbs 13:14). What if we have many advantages in our lives but not wisdom? If we have love but not wisdom, we will harm people with the best of intentions. If we have courage but not wisdom, we will blunder boldly. If we have truth but not wisdom, we will make the gospel ugly to other people. If we have technology but not wisdom, we will use the best communications ever invented to broadcast stupidity. If we have revival but not wisdom, we'll use the power of God to throw the church into reverse gear. Jonathan Edwards wrote during the First Great Awakening, "When the devil finds he can keep men quiet and [complacent] no longer, then he drives them to excesses and extravagances. He holds them back as long as he can; but when he can do it no longer, then he will push them on and, if possible, run them upon their heads."[2] But wisdom knows how to spread the gospel with no embarrassing regrets.

Wisdom is the grace of Christ beautifying our daily lives. Paul said that

God has "lavished" his grace upon us "in all wisdom and insight" (Ephesians 1:7, 8). God's grace is smart grace. The Bible says that in Christ are hidden "all the treasures of wisdom and knowledge" (Colossians 2:3). The wise way to live is not always obvious or intuitive or popular. It is hidden. Here's where it is hidden: "We preach Christ crucified . . . the wisdom of God" (1 Corinthians 1:23, 24).

We must understand that there are two kinds of wisdom, and they are competing for our trust. The Bible calls them "the wisdom from above" and "the wisdom that . . . is earthly, unspiritual, demonic" (James 3:15, 17). Do you remember what Jesus said to Peter when Peter urged him not to go to the cross? Peter was saying, "Look, boss, there's another way to go about this. Crosses are not a smart formula for success." But Jesus said to Peter, "Get behind me, Satan! . . . For you are not setting your mind on the things of God, but on the things of man" (Matthew 16:21–23). How did Peter earn that stunning rebuke? Not by setting his mind on the things of Satan but just on the things of man—natural, understandable things, like survival. Peter was being wise with the wisdom that is earthly, unspiritual, demonic. Our natural wisdom panders to our pride and makes losing unthinkable. But J. R. R. Tolkien's Ring Trilogy reminds us that our golden rings of power only make us weird, like Gollum. The key to life is not getting more of these golden rings but throwing them decisively away into the fires of Mount Doom. That humility is "the wisdom from above."

> Ah! God is other than we think, his ways are far above,
> Far beyond reason's height and reached only by childlike love.
>
> Then learn to scorn the praise of men, and learn to lose with God,
> For Jesus won the world through shame and beckons thee his road.[3]

That is the wisdom of the cross. That wisdom frees us from the distortions of our pride and opens the way to resurrection and new life. In *The Pilgrim's Regress*, C. S. Lewis says the path of wisdom leads through a valley: "'And what is this valley called?' 'We call it now simply Wisdom's Valley; but the oldest maps mark it as the Valley of Humiliation.'"[4]

There is irony here. The wisdom of Proverbs started out historically for the training of leaders in ancient Israel.[5] It was written by kings and others in the royal court for young men in their teens and twenties whose future was bright with nobility. But we rise to that greatness and leadership and influence not our way, not by our natural strategies, but God's way, through the cross, through humility. An old poem says:

When God wants to drill a man
And thrill a man
And skill a man
When God wants to mold a man
To play the noblest part

When He yearns with all His heart
To create so great and bold a man
That all the world shall be amazed,
Watch His methods, watch His ways!

How He ruthlessly perfects
Whom He royally elects!
How He hammers him and hurts him
And with mighty blows converts him
Into shapes and forms of clay
Which only God can understand

How He bends but never breaks
When his good He undertakes
How He uses whom He chooses
And with mighty power infuses him
With every act induces him
To try His splendor out—
God knows what He's about.

Wisdom is the gospel of Christ reshaping us for royalty, as God places us on his anvil and we trust him enough to stay there until his work is done.

Here is how the book of Proverbs is designed. It is an anthology—that is, a collection of writings from several authors. Solomon is listed as the author, because he contributed the most and because he's the famous one. But after the title in 1:1—"The proverbs of Solomon, son of David, king of Israel"—then the purpose of the book is stated in 1:2–6. That's where we find out what God will accomplish in us through this book. The theme or motto of the book is famously stated in 1:7: "The fear of the LORD is the beginning of knowledge; fools despise wisdom and instruction." Then the rest of chapters 1—9 is a series of poems selling wisdom to us, motivating us to get into the book and receive its teachings with an eager heart. Chapters 1—9 make the case as to why we should care. Then look at 10:1, where we read, "The proverbs of Solomon." This is where the proverbs as such begin. Chapters 1—9 are all introductory. They are connected discourses, rather like psalms. But when the proverbs themselves begin in chapter 10, the style changes. Instead of lengthy, unified sections, each verse is its own tiny unit. So after chapters 1—9 I will bring together various proverbs that address wisdom-issues in our lives—for example, how to use money, how to be a family, how to use words, and so forth. All the proverbs from 10:1—22:16 come from Solomon himself. Then in Proverbs 22:17 we read, "Incline your ear, and hear the words of the wise." Proverbs 22:17—24:22 is the next collection within the anthology. This section is known as The Thirty Sayings of the Wise. Then in Proverbs 24:23, the next collection begins: "These also are sayings of the wise," and that brief section runs through verse 34 of that chapter. Then in 25:1—29:27 we have more proverbs of Solomon: "These also are proverbs of Solomon which the men of Hezekiah king of Judah copied" (25:1). The last two collections in the book are "The words of Agur son of Jakeh. The oracle" (30:1–33) and "The words of King Lemuel. An oracle that his mother taught him" (31:1–31). So there are seven major sections in the book of Proverbs—the introduction in chapters 1—9, followed by six collections of proverbs by Solomon and other divinely inspired geniuses.

What then is at stake for you and me in the book of Proverbs? Why does this book deserve our endless fascination? T. S. Eliot spoke to our times when he asked these questions:

> Where is the life we have lost in living?
> Where is the wisdom we have lost in knowledge?
> Where is the knowledge we have lost in information?[6]

In our chaotic lives of constant stop-start-stop-start short-attention-span mental habits, with an endless stream of momentarily visible Twitter-feed fragments of information, we have been reduced to one splinter factoid after another, and we are trying to patch together some kind of elegant whole worth living. That is difficult. But the problem is not just that we are fidgety and distracted; it's that our information, however much we have, is no basis for a life. We need Jesus to rescue us from our information and even from our knowledge. We need Jesus to counsel us with a new (and yet ancient) wisdom that comes from him. Then we can live. That is what is at stake here—our living rather than our dying. And Christ speaks to us for our living calmly, patiently, lovingly, seriously through the book of Proverbs.

This book works when we deliberately slow down and listen and think and journal and pray. For many years Billy Graham read one chapter of the book of Proverbs every day in order each month, because there are 31 chapters in the book.[7] We need that too. In his article "Is Google Making Us Stupid?" Nicholas Carr helps us to see how we are being changed and therefore how we need to change back:

As the media theorist Marshall McLuhan pointed out in the 1960s, media are not just passive channels of information. They supply the stuff of thought, but they also shape the process of thought. And what the Net seems to be doing is chipping away my capacity for concentration and contemplation. My mind now expects to take in information the way the Net distributes it: in a swiftly moving stream of particles. Once I was a scuba diver in the sea of words. Now I zip along the surface like a guy on a Jet Ski.[8]

It is time to get off our information high, pick up the Bible, and go deep. But the biggest challenge is not in our surroundings. It is internal to ourselves. We bring a precondition into our counseling sessions with Jesus.

The book of Proverbs uses a certain Hebrew word to describe us as we start out. It is the word *petî*.[9] It shows up in our English Bibles as "simple" (ESV), "naive" (NASB), "ignorant" (JB). We do not like being told we are simple, naive, and ignorant. But we can put away our feeling of insult and be glad, because the Bible does not idealize us. The Bible sets the bar low, where beginners like us can get traction and succeed. I am reminded of my sixth grade report card from Allendale Elementary School, Pasadena, California, 1960-61, which I have before me now. Mrs. Karpé was my long-suffering teacher. How was I doing? Reading, C. Math, C-. Social Studies, D. Art, C. Work and Study Habits, C-. Mrs. Karpé's written comment was:

Buddy is not working up to grade level requirement. He has a tendency to procrastinate, lose his work, then panics. He has a promising "potential," but I would like to see him exercise it, do something about it.

In response to which my dad wrote in the following space for the parent's comments:

Buddy is going to take a far greater interest in all of his work at school. Please give us a progress report in one month. We will contact you. Thanks for your interest.

I was a *petî*. And the proof of it was not my age or even my performance but just that I didn't much care. But in God's mercy I had a teacher and a dad who did care. I am thankful because "No one left to himself ever arrives at wisdom."[10]

This word *petî* is related to a Hebrew verb that means "to be open." A *petî* keeps his options open. He is uncommitted. He may even see himself as above commitment. But it gets him into trouble: "The prudent sees danger and hides himself, but the simple go on and suffer for it" (Proverbs

22:3; 27:12). Why does a *petî* keep doing that? Because he does not *want* to make up his mind and commit himself: "How long, O simple ones, will you *love* being simple?" (Proverbs 1:22). Martyn Lloyd-Jones drills down into our problem:

> You will never make yourself feel that you are a sinner, because there is a mechanism in you as a result of sin that will always be defending you against every accusation. We are all on very good terms with ourselves, and we can always put up a good case for ourselves. Even if we try to make ourselves feel that we are sinners, we will never do it. There is only one way to know that we are sinners, and that is to have some dim, glimmering conception of God.[11]

Until we come alive to God, it seems cool to stand aloof and laugh at everything. It feels superior. But it is foolish, because we are not neutral. We do not have our little devilish nature sitting on one shoulder tempting us and our little angelic nature sitting on the other shoulder restraining us. We have no angel. We have only a devil of a heart telling us we are angels, and we believe it. That guilty naiveté about ourselves is how we are born. It's why we hate correction. Theologians call it Original Sin, and it is very real. We need Jesus to save us, first and foremost, from not needing to be saved.

As we launch our study of Proverbs, let's so humble ourselves that we are enthusiastic about Jesus saving us from ourselves. We are born proud and defensive. It makes us negative, whiny, suspicious, unsatisfiable, squandering our opportunity in life. But then we are reborn by grace into newness and repentance and freedom as we listen to our Wonderful Counselor who loves us better than we love ourselves. That new humility is "the fear of the LORD" and "the beginning of wisdom" (Proverbs 9:10). That is how we begin our journey into wisdom, and it remains a lifelong, moment-by-moment attitude adjustment:

> Believers may not often realize it, but even as believers we are either centered on man or centered on God. There is no alternative. Either God is the center of our universe and we have become rightly adjusted to him, or we have made ourselves the center and are attempting to make all else orbit around us and for us.[12]

Even in the small things of everyday life, Christ wants to be our true center. Then we learn to be wise. Then we really start to live.

In Proverbs 9, the elegant Lady Wisdom and the seductive Woman Folly are standing on either side of the road calling out, "Whoever is simple, let him turn in here!" (Proverbs 9:4, 16). What happens to us if we turn toward Folly? We start down a path from being a *petî* to becoming hardened into a "scoffer" who cannot come back. "A scoffer seeks wisdom in vain" (Proverbs 14:6).

What happens to us if we commit to Wisdom? "The path of life leads upward for the wise; they leave the grave behind" (Proverbs 15:24, NLT). True wisdom is walking further with Jesus than we've ever gone before, further than we've ever dreamed of going. It is not risky. All we leave behind is the grave. All we leave behind is our stupidity and futility and ultimate damnation. But his path is marked by promise every step of the way. Here is his promise to every fool who chooses the way of his cross: "He who began a good work in you will bring it to completion at the day of Jesus Christ" (Philippians 1:6).

Let's walk his way together.

2

Let's Begin

PROVERBS 1:1–7

The fear of the Lord is the beginning of knowledge.

1:7

IN OUR DAILY LIVES we need more than rules. Sometimes life is too complex for a simple rule. We need wisdom to fill in the blanks moment by moment, and God gives us his wisdom in the book of Proverbs. But we need wisdom for another reason. It is possible to live by all the rules and be ugly about it. We have all known people who were blameless, in their way, and we disliked them. But wisdom "will bestow on you a beautiful crown" (Proverbs 4:9). We want Jesus to place that crown on our heads, for his sake. Wise Christians and wise churches become radiantly attractive. The Bible says, "Walk in wisdom toward outsiders" (Colossians 4:5). How? More people are won for Christ by beauty than by rules.

We begin our journey deeper into God's wisdom at Proverbs 1:1–7. The word "beginning" is seen in verse 7: "The fear of the LORD is the beginning of knowledge." Everyone needs a new beginning with God. That is why we go to church and pray and receive the gospel. We want what only God can do for us, and the fear of the Lord is how we receive it. The fear of the Lord is both a doorway and a pathway. It is a new beginning, and it never ends. You can begin afresh with God today. You can say to him, "Lord, I know the rules fairly well. But the beauty of wisdom takes me much further with you. I want to go there." You can walk through that doorway and get going on that pathway. The only price you will pay is letting God be God to you.

Proverbs 1:1–7 opens up the whole book. It divides this way: first, the title of the book, in verse 1; second, the goals of the book, in verses 2–6; third, the threshold of the book, in verse 7.

The Title

> The proverbs of Solomon, son of David, king of Israel. (Proverbs 1:1)

Two things stand out here: one, how this book communicates; two, where this book comes from.

One: how this book communicates: "The proverbs." Proverbs are the literary strategy of this book. What is a proverb? In English a proverb is a short saying of practical truth that's easy to remember, like "Look before you leap" or "A stitch in time saves nine." Biblical proverbs are sound-bite-ish too, but they offer a lot more than common sense.

What then is a Biblical proverb? The Hebrew noun "proverb" is related to a verb that means "to represent, to be like." So a proverb is a little model of reality, a little verbal representation of some aspect of our daily lives. And by picking a proverb up and turning it over and over and looking at it from all angles, we can see something about our lives before we step out into the actual reality. The world says, Live and learn. God is saying, Learn and live.[1]

Think of a proverb this way. When the Wright brothers flew their airplane for the first time in 1903, they knew it would take off. How did they know? They had built a wind tunnel where they tested different wing designs before they risked their necks in actual flight. That is what the proverbs are for. We can explore a real-life situation within the virtual reality of a proverb. We can know in advance what is going to fly and what is going to crash. Biblical wisdom tells us what life is really like.

Two: where this book comes from: ". . . of Solomon, son of David, king of Israel." One of the fascinating things about the book of Proverbs is that it does not often connect with the history of God's people. Over and over the Bible calls us back to Abraham and Moses and the exodus and so forth. But the book of Proverbs does not do that. Not only so, but Proverbs 22:17—24:22 does parallel aspects of "The Instruction of Amenemope" from Egypt.[2] This is why some scholars perceive the wisdom of Proverbs as accessible without God. They see this wisdom as available to everyone in the same way—by being smart enough. And indeed we can learn from the best practices of smart people who do not claim Jesus. But the wisdom of Proverbs comes from "Solomon, son of David, king of Israel." Right up front, the book tells us it stands in the flow of Biblical history, which leads us to Jesus. Here is the point: The fear of the Lord Jesus Christ is the beginning of *this* wisdom.

What did Solomon understand that made such a difference? He connected the Lord with real life, all of it. First Kings 4:29–34 tells us that Solomon was a Renaissance man. He was fascinated by *everything*. He studied plants, from the cedars of Lebanon to the hyssop that grows out of a crack in a wall. He studied animals. He composed music. He did not compartmentalize God. He understood that everything is connected with our Creator, and therefore everything is interesting. Solomon was like Jonathan Edwards, who saw divine glory all around him. Here is how Edwards perceived reality:

> God had created lower things to be signs that pointed to higher spiritual realities. The universe, then, was a complex language of God. Nothing in it was accidental. Everything pointed to a higher meaning. Scripture . . . was the key to reading the true meaning of everything else.[3]

The Biblical worldview opens up the higher meaning of money and sex and power and everything across the landscape of our lives. And we "get it" not by outsmarting someone else but by fearing the Lord. Solomon did. So can you, by God's grace. Just let God be God to you.

The Goals

To know wisdom and instruction,
    to understand words of insight,
to receive instruction in wise dealing,
    in righteousness, justice, and equity;
to give prudence to the simple,
    knowledge and discretion to the youth—
Let the wise hear and increase in learning,
    and the one who understands obtain guidance—[4]
to understand a proverb and a saying,
    the words of the wise and their riddles. (Proverbs 1:2–6)

God has two goals for us in the book of Proverbs. Verse 2 states them. One is deep character, and the other is straight thinking. "To know wisdom and instruction"—that's deep character. "To understand words of insight"— that's straight thinking. Verses 3, 4 tell us more about deep character, and verse 6 tells us more about straight thinking. Verse 5 is a parenthesis, urging even wise people to keep growing. Everybody can take a new step with the Lord—the simple, the youthful, the wise. Everybody can be on a growth edge together. We can be a community of growing people.

What about God's first purpose for us—deep character? "To know wisdom and instruction," verse 2 says. We haven't defined wisdom yet, so now is the time. What does the sage mean by "wisdom"? Wisdom is more than brains. It is more than morals. We could memorize the whole Bible, and mean it from the heart, without wisdom. Wisdom is skill, expertise, competence that understands how life really works, how to achieve successful and even beautiful results. We see a picture of wisdom in Exodus 35:31, where the word translated "wisdom" in Proverbs 1:2 is used for the skill of an artist adorning the tabernacle. We see wisdom in Jeremiah 10:9 where the expertise of goldsmiths is called "the work of skilled men," or wise men. We see wisdom in Psalm 107:27 for the know-how of sailors, who use the winds and tides to make their way through the sea to their destination. Whether craftsmanship working with the materials of life or seamanship steering through the currents of life, so to speak, wisdom understands how real life can work well. Wisdom knows better than to walk onto the football field and hope the game will go well somehow; wisdom draws up a game plan that will score more touchdowns than the opponents because that plan takes into account not only the rules of the game but also psychology and timing and strategy and everything it takes to win. That is wisdom.

This is seen all through the Bible. *Perceiving wisdom* asks the hard questions about life and understands God's answers. *Acting wisdom* guides us in our practical conduct every day. *Communicating wisdom* educates us in the school of the sages, as we see here in Proverbs 1:2–6.[5] We are being invited into the counsels of the best and the brightest.

Now if wisdom is so desirable, and it is, then why isn't everyone running toward wisdom? Why is it rare? Because of the next word in verse 2: "instruction." It is also translated "discipline" (NLT). Sorry, friends, but we are not born wise. We get into wisdom the hard way, through the Lord's instruction and discipline, through being chastened and corrected. We do not like that. It is humiliating. It is hard to admit we are wrong. But we make progress in wisdom to the extent that we are teachable. I like how C. J. Mahaney put it in his book on humility: "I'm a proud man pursuing humility by the grace of God."[6] We are foolish people pursuing wisdom by humbling ourselves under the Lord's correction. Can any of us be above it? When we are honest enough with God to change, he puts that crown of beauty on our heads. It is what he wants to do.

Verse 3 is how we start. It is written from the learner's point of view— "to receive instruction." That word "receive" is the key that unlocks the door. The Bible says, "Receive with meekness the implanted word, which is able to save your souls" (James 1:21). That simple humility, that openness, is how we gain velocity in wise dealing, righteousness, justice, and equity—all so beautiful and powerful.

Verse 4 shifts to the teacher's point of view: "to give prudence to the simple, knowledge and discretion to the youth." The simple, the young, gain three benefits from wisdom, according to verse 4. First, "prudence." Do you like that word? I don't. It seems so Victorian. It reminds me of the Beatles' *White Album* and "Dear Prudence":

> Dear Prudence, won't you come out to play?
> Dear Prudence, greet the brand new day
> The sun is up, the sky is blue
> It's beautiful and so are you
> Dear Prudence, won't you come out to play?

She needed to have some fun! Is there another translation of this Hebrew word? Yes, there is: "shrewdness" (NRSV). I like that word. And it is faithful to the Hebrew text. Shrewdness is a good kind of cunning. In this world we need that. Shrewdness is tactics that succeed when so much is on the line.

Second, "knowledge." What does everyone need to know? The very thing our popular theories deny, namely, that there is an inescapable link between deed and consequence. We think we can create our own designer lives, even new selves, by force of raw choice. But the truth is, reality is not made-to-order. We cannot make it up as we go. We were born into a preexisting order that God created long ago. We need to know what that order is and how it works in relationships, in finances, in sex, in every area of life, so that we can stop shooting ourselves in the foot. If we know, we can adjust, and we can thrive.

Third, "discretion." That is the caginess that sees through the temptations coming at us every day, for example, through advertising. God wants to give us the deep character that can't be fooled anymore. He can help us outfox our temptations.

Verses 3, 4 are how we start out, as beginners. Verse 5 tells us that even seasoned veterans can keep on learning: "Let the wise hear and increase in learning, and the one who understands obtain guidance." Let's be realistic about ourselves—as we age, it can be harder to stay fresh and expectant and moving forward on an upward trajectory of growth. It is easy to stall, it is easy to coast. We can get lazy. But let's not die before we die! Fight for open-mindedness and honesty and discovery and newness of life. Stay humble and keep learning. The Apostle Paul did. Even in his final days, he wanted to keep reading and studying and learning (2 Timothy 4:6, 13). That's how we can be a blessing to younger people too.

God wants to give every one of us deep character. That is the first of his two purposes in this book. His second purpose is straight thinking. Look back to the second line of verse 2: "to understand words of insight." What does God have for us here? Think of the difference between Sherlock Holmes and Dr. Watson. You know how a client would walk into Holmes's apartment at 221B Baker Street and Sherlock Holmes could take one look and know nineteen things about him, and it was always "Elementary, my dear Watson." Dr. Watson saw the same person, but not with the same insight. This word "insight" means that the non-obvious can become obvious to you. The immature might not see what you see. They might even misunderstand you. This happens often between parents and children. But, parents, it is your role to be the Sherlock Holmes of your family. Don't surrender that to your kids. They don't have enough insight yet. They need yours.

Verse 6 tells us more about straight thinking: "to understand a proverb and a saying, the words of the wise and their riddles." Picture it this way. As we come to the book of Proverbs, we are approaching a community of wisdom, a group of people standing around talking together, men and women, who are Yoda-smart. We beginners sidle up to this circle of amazing people. We see, there in the circle of "the wise," Solomon and Isaiah and Paul and Augustine and Luther and other remarkable people we have known personally and admired. We start listening to the conversation going on inside that circle. We overhear words and concepts we do not understand at first, so we have to stick with it to catch on. But as we do, we begin to leave behind our shallow entertainment mindset with its effortless, pat answers that in fact have always failed us. As we listen to the wise, we grow. We, even we, become profound people too. The final reason for this, of course, is not us, and not even them. According to verse 7, *God* is there. The wise are letting God be God to them.

The Threshold

> The fear of the LORD is the beginning of knowledge;
>   fools despise wisdom and instruction. (Proverbs 1:7)

Verse 7 is the theme of the book of Proverbs. If we distilled the whole book into one drop, it would be verse 7. What is the fear of the Lord? The structure of this verse is itself suggestive. Hebrew poetry was written in parallel lines—an A-line, then a B-line, and the B-line clarifies the A-line. So how does the second line help us here? The key is the word "despise." That is an emotional word, a word of contempt and relational aloofness. It is the arrogance of being above instruction, too smart for it, too good for it, too busy for it. Such a "fool" might be a gifted person, but he does not "feel the need for moral cleansing."[7] What then is the fear of the Lord? It is not a cringing dread before the Lord. It is not a guilty "Oh no, here comes God. I'm in for it now." The fear of the Lord is openness to him, eagerness to please him, humility to be instructed by him (Proverbs 15:33).[8] The fear of the Lord is a willingness to turn from evil and change (Job 28:28). The fear of the Lord is surrender to his will (Genesis 22:12). The fear of the Lord is one way we love him (Deuteronomy 6:2, 5). The fear of Christ is meekly fitting in with one another (Ephesians 5:21, literally translated). The fear of the Lord is when we realize, "I am not the measure of all things. I am being measured." That reverence toward God, perhaps surprisingly, builds our confidence and flows out as a "fountain of life" into everyone and everything we care about (Proverbs 14:26, 27). It takes us to that place of maturity where no one has to follow us around with a tedious list of do's and don't's, constantly telling us what to do. We are motivated from deep within. We know what is right, and it is what we love, because it is of God.

This wonderful fear of the Lord is where we begin our journey into wisdom. It is how we keep making progress all the way. It opens our eyes, and it keeps them open. C. S. Lewis wrote:

> In God you come up against something which is in every respect immeasurably superior to yourself. Unless you know God as that—and, therefore, know yourself as nothing in comparison—you do not know God at all. As long as you are proud, you cannot know God. A proud man is always looking down on things and people; and, of course, as long as you are looking down, you cannot see something that is above you.[9]

That realism runs opposite to the dominant thinking of our modern age. In his *Discourse on Method*, Descartes famously wrote, "I think, therefore I am."[10] He wanted certainty. He wanted to know what is real. So he did what seemed obvious. He started doubting everything, to find out what would be left. He whittled away at everything until he noticed that he was still there, he was real, the one doubting. He could not doubt that: "I think [that is, doubt], therefore I am." So Descartes, the father of modern thought, started rebuilding reality outward from himself. For over 300 years our culture has been trying to live that way, building our civilization and our personal lives on ourselves. It has failed. Absolutizing our own capacity for generating knowledge and hope and certainty exposes us to self-deception, as postmodernism has shown. The autonomous Self cannot create certainty, much less beauty, but it certainly can be fooled. Every one of us is living proof of that.

The Bible reverses Descartes: "The fear of the LORD is the beginning of knowledge." Knowledge starts within God, and then it moves toward us. He must reveal it by grace, and we must receive it in humility. Verse 7 is saying that what your ABC's are to reading Shakespeare, what playing the scales are to performing Bach, what $2 + 2 = 4$ is to doing calculus, the fear of the Lord is to wisdom. We start there, and we never leave it behind. Our search for reality can go wrong not only because of miscalculations along the way but also because of one grand blunder at the start—leaving God out, and making ourselves the judges of everything.[11]

But it can be extremely painful to learn the fear of the Lord. It is death to our narcissistic egos and self-assured opinions and superior neutrality. But we do not change for the better by turning inward. We change as we turn outward and upward to the Lord with an awakened sense of his sheer reality, his moral beauty, his eternal grandeur, infinitely above us but relevant to us. Our true crisis is not informational but relational. It is *he*, the risen and living Lord Jesus Christ, to whom we must pay close attention, if we are ever going to learn anything. That means we must forsake the fool within, named Self, decisively and endlessly. "Change of being, *metanoia*, is not brought about by straining and 'will-power' but by a long deep process of unselfing."[12] There is no other way.

Wise people humbly revere God and lovingly live to please him. Mr. Beaver explained why: "Safe? Who said anything about safe? "'Course he isn't safe. But he's good. He's the King, I tell you."[13] Do you revere God that way? Have you experienced how freeing it is to humble yourself before your superior, Jesus Christ? Getting down low before him—that is where we all belong. It is not degrading. It is profound. Remember *The Wind in the Willows*, when Rat and Mole go looking for the baby otter and stumble into the presence of God:

> Suddenly the Mole felt a great Awe fall upon him, an awe that turned his muscles to water, bowed his head, and rooted his feet to the ground. It was no panic terror—indeed, he felt wonderfully at peace and happy. . . .
> "Rat!" he found breath to whisper, shaking. "Are you afraid?"
> "Afraid?" murmured the Rat, his eyes shining with unutterable love. "Afraid! Of *Him*? O, never, never! And yet—and yet—O, Mole, I am afraid!"
> Then the two animals, crouching to the earth, bowed their heads and did worship.[14]

If you would like to experience God with that humility, here is how you can. You look at the cross. You see a wise man hanging there, dying in the place of fools like you, because he loves you. You may despise him, but he does not despise you. You may be above him, but he humbled himself for you. Look there at him. Look away from yourself. Look at him, and keep looking until your pride melts. You will not only worship, you will begin to grow wise.

3

Violence!

PROVERBS 1:8–19

My son, if sinners entice you . . .

1:10

THE BIBLE DOES NOT DESCRIBE how life *ought* to be. It matches how life *is*. The wisdom of Proverbs is reality-based counseling as we live in this fantasy-world of human invention. We see the blunt realism of the Bible in Proverbs 1:8–19.

Why are we in the book of Proverbs at all? Because so much of life is a series of nuanced judgment calls. The Ten Commandments say, "You shall not murder" (Exodus 20:13). Are you struggling with that decision today? Probably not. But even at this moment we are all creating social dynamics both subtle and powerful, and those dynamics are either life-depleting or life-enriching. What makes the difference is the wisdom of our life together as the church of Christ. Have you ever done something with the best of intentions, but then it exploded in your face—like pathetic Wile E. Coyote in the Road Runner cartoons? Good intentions and wishful thinking can be oblivious to reality. But wisdom helps us create the chemistry—not rules but chemistry[1]—of life at its best together in the new community of Christ.

Wisdom does not theorize. Wisdom pays attention to the realities built into us by God our Creator. Wisdom humbly gives in to God's design; it adapts and adjusts. A wise person notices, picks up on the clues, cuts with the grain, tears along the perforated line. Unwise people can be gifted, but they are trying to be healthy on junk food, or run high RPMs on low-octane gas, or get home by the wrong road, or swim against the stream of the universe. Sin is trying to succeed by ignoring reality. And that makes the devil the ultimate fool. He wants to reengineer the creation his own way. He is both evil and dumb. C. S. Lewis wrote, "The Devil is (in the long run) an ass."[2] But the book of Proverbs is where God speaks to us as our life coach, guiding us into the only real success that's out there.

In Proverbs 1:8–19 we hear two voices—the wisdom that is reality-based and the folly that is in denial. Wisdom is speaking here as a loving father. Fools are speaking here too. Their message is a kind of reverse-evangelism. They are inviting us into their dead-end lives. But God is calling us into the beauty of real human relationships. Here is what God is saying in this passage: *Refuse violence. It is tempting, but it will destroy you. Wisdom will beautify you.*

But hold on here. Violence? That is a bad thing, we all know. But why is that message here? Has anyone *ever* said to you, "Come with us, let us lie in wait for blood" (v. 11)? In certain neighborhoods, that might happen. But still, this passage can seem surprising. As we have already seen, the book of Proverbs opens with a mini-introduction in 1:1–7, and then the rest of chapters 1—9 is the mega-introduction. Chapters 1—9 are a series of poems in praise of wisdom, preparing us for the actual proverbs in chapters 10—31. So, now we come to 1:8. We probably come to this verse thinking, "Okay, Mr. Super-Smart Wise Man, we're ready. Tell us the positive difference wisdom can make in our lives." And the first thing he says is, "Don't join a gang!" Why *that*? Let's get inside this and dig out the wisdom. There are three points here: the offer of wisdom, the warning of wisdom, and the promise of wisdom.

The Offer of Wisdom

> Hear, my son, your father's instruction,
>   and forsake not your mother's teaching,
> for they are a graceful garland for your head
>   and pendants for your neck. (1:8, 9)

God is speaking to us through a father advising his son. Every dad needs to have some talks with his son during the critical teen years. That is the environment that shaped this wisdom originally. Now, embedded in the Biblical book of Proverbs, it speaks to us all. But a dad is looking his boy straight in the eye and saying, "Son, here's the kind of world you're going to be living in every day of your life. Here's what you can expect. And here's what you have to do about it." That is a wise dad. He is not shielding his boy from the real world. He is telling him about it in advance, but in a way that will help his son rather than degrade him. He does not take his son to see a gangster movie, which is fantasy anyway. He tells his son the truth.

We are in a family, too, in the church. That kind of family is worth a lot today. Some of us were under-parented. But God our Father loves us by locating us inside his family, where we have father-figures, we have spiritual mothers, and all of us are growing together.

How is our heavenly Father counseling us in verses 8, 9? He is saying, "If you'll listen to me, my wisdom will make you *attractive*." Why are most people not in church on a Sunday morning? Because they do not see churches as attractive. But here is what God wants us to see. He did not make us for mediocrity. He made us for glory. And he gets us there through wisdom. God's wisdom is beautiful, impressive. He puts a garland on our head and pendants on our neck. What do those metaphors mean? A garland was a victor's wreath. In chapter 4 the garland stands in parallel with "a beautiful crown" (Proverbs 4:9). And a pendant was a chain around one's neck as a mark of prestige. Think of an Olympic gold medal.

The gospel says, "Put on the Lord Jesus Christ" (Romans 13:14). So we take off the rags of pettiness, and we put on the humility of Jesus, which is winsome. Anyone can sniff out the difference between someone who is proud and self-important and someone who is kind and sincere—and which one is *esteemed*? Our Father is offering to put his glory upon us. A big part of the spreading power of the gospel is the wisdom God puts on believers and on their church. The Bible says, "We aim at what is honorable not only in the Lord's sight but also in the sight of man" (2 Corinthians 8:21). The Bible says, "Let your reasonableness be known to everyone" (Philippians 4:5). I love that word "reasonableness." It is the opposite of being trigger-happy and harsh and censorious. It means being fair, especially toward those who disagree with you. In this angry world, such reasonableness is impressive. God is saying to us, "May I put that pendant around your neck?" And we are saying, "Yes, please do." We want the people of our city, as they visit our church, to walk away saying, "I don't agree with everything they believe, but those people are fair. They are not out for themselves. I'm attracted." We do not put that wreath on our heads. God does—and then other people do. Here is our part: "I try to please everyone in everything I do, not seeking my own advantage" (1 Corinthians 10:33). That wisdom takes us way beyond crossing T's and dotting I's. Technical rule-keeping can be ugly. But there is nothing degrading in Christ. He is a classy person, and humbly listening to him rubs off on us.

The Warning of Wisdom

> My son, if sinners entice you,
>   do not consent.
> If they say, "Come with us, let us lie in wait for blood;
>   let us ambush the innocent without reason;
> like Sheol let us swallow them alive,
>   and whole, like those who go down to the pit;
> we shall find all precious goods,
>   we shall fill our houses with plunder;
> throw in your lot among us;
>   we will all have one purse"—
> my son, do not walk in the way with them;
>   hold back your foot from their paths,
> for their feet run to evil,
>   and they make haste to shed blood.
> For in vain is a net spread
>   in the sight of any bird,
> but these men lie in wait for their own blood;
>   they set an ambush for their own lives.
> Such are the ways of everyone who is greedy for unjust gain;
>   it takes away the life of its possessors. (1:10–19)

Let's understand two things here. First, who the "sinners" are: "My son, if *sinners* entice you . . . " Every one of us is a sinner. Even the wise father-figure speaking here is a sinner. So who are "the sinners" he is warning us against? The structure of this Hebrew noun suggests habitual, chronic sinners.[3] In the extreme, this kind of person is a professional criminal, like the bad guys in *The Godfather*. Bullying is how some people make their way through the world. The key to this human profile is anyone who gets ahead by his own devices, anyone who is out for number one. They are the "sinners" of whom we must be aware. They are out there. You will encounter them.

Secondly, note how this scenario actually plays out in our lives. This father is not wasting his breath. He is telling his son, "When people like this come to you, not *if* they do but *when* they do, here's what you do . . . " I wonder if you dads are having that kind of talk with your sons. The father-figure in our passage knows what his son will experience, and he warns him. What do all of us inevitably run into? If not an urban gang, how can this scenario play out for you and me?

In many ways. Look at verse 19: "Such are the ways of *everyone* who is greedy for unjust gain." The father broadens the relevance of his message to everyone who fits this description: "greedy for unjust gain." That includes money, of course, but more. At its core, unjust gain succeeds by stepping on someone else. Along the way we will meet people like this—self-centered, narcissistic back-stabbers. They can show up in many forms in our world. For starters:

- bullies at school ganging up on another kid, tormenting him or her to the point of despair
- computer hackers stealing people's identity and money
- Wall Street insiders exploiting the system for their own selfish gain
- political "good old boys" neglecting their constituents but taking care of each other
- Islamic terrorists plotting and murdering people to create their own ideal Muslim world
- class-motivated revolutionaries taking their revenge on the privileged wealthy, to punish historic wrongs
- racists treating others as non-persons who just don't count and can be disposed of or held down forever
- political candidates stealing elections and defrauding the voters because winning, not serving, is the goal
- Mao Tse-tung's China, Joseph Stalin's Russia, Adolf Hitler's Germany, Pol Pot's Cambodia, and others—the murderous modern state[4]
- neighbors who *need* bad things to be true of someone else in order to justify themselves, gossiping that person's reputation to death
- intellectuals who rationalize violence in pursuit of their social utopias[5]
- office politics bringing the CEO down, or faculty politics bringing the Dean down
- a faction splitting a church. And it only takes one person to get it going. But "if anyone destroys God's temple, God will destroy him" (1 Corinthians 3:17).

The list could go on and on. There are many legal, polite, arguable, even religious ways of saying, "Come with us, let us lie in wait for blood." But what is this all about? Pride, envy, greed, jealousy, retaliation, and so forth. Deep in every heart is a kind of blood-lust. Do not trust your own sense of injury. It can be sinful, in part anyway. The test is this: Are you happy when other people succeed? Or are you happy when they get their comeuppance? Do you pray for your persecutors to be blessed or to be punished? A British newspaper described our hearts like this:

> There is no vice of which a man can be guilty, no meanness, no shabbiness, no unkindness, which excites so much indignation among his contemporaries, friends and neighbors, as his success. This is the one unpardonable crime. . . . The man who writes as we cannot write, who speaks as we cannot speak, labors as we cannot labor, thrives as we cannot thrive, has accumulated on his own person all the offenses of which man can be guilty. Down with him![6]

Have you ever felt that envy and resentment deep inside? It is where violence begins. Your heart is lying in wait for blood. When this rage pops up to the surface, observe yourself carefully. You will probably recruit others to your cause. Sin tends to recruit. Watch those thoughts and feelings creeping into conversations with other people. You will want to get others on your side. Look at verse 14: "Throw in your lot among us; we will all have one purse." A cause, even a negative cause, provides a group to belong to. It is one way we nurse our grudges, and it feels good. But whenever we gather around grievance rather than Jesus, that is counterfeit community, black-market relationships, and that negativity is on a collision course with reality. It cannot succeed long-term. Connect these two: "Come with us, let us lie in wait for blood" (v. 11), and "We will all have one purse" (v. 14). Don't you see? "Help us slit his throat, but we'll take care of you!" How long can *that* hold together? God is warning us here. Sure, we all long for community. But there is a kind of community to which we should never want to belong. Rather, let's consider God's alternative, a safe community freely open to all through the grace of our violently crucified Christ.

The Promise of Wisdom

Blessed are the peacemakers, for they shall be called sons of God. (Matthew 5:9)

The night Jesus was born, the angels shouted, "On earth peace" (Luke 2:14). The night before Jesus died he said, "My peace I leave with you. . . . Not as the world gives do I give to you" (John 14.27). The Bible says of his peace, "Let the peace of Christ rule in your hearts" (Colossians 3:15). When we press the gospel into our hearts as authoritative to rule, believing this good news that God has come to us not in attack-mode but as our peacemaker—that's when we no longer feel on edge, and we become peacemakers, *shalom*-makers. Then others will perceive us as sons of God. In the Old Testament sons of wickedness are wicked people (2 Samuel 3:34). So, sons of God are Godlike people. They are wise and beautiful, with garlands and pendants of grace. The gospel does that to us.

Here is how you go there and live and thrive there. God has made peace with you through Christ. God is not plotting against you. He is not taking aim. His finger is not on the trigger. *He is not lying in wait for your blood. He gave his own at the cross.* Believe it. Receive it. Put that truth on your heart every day, and he will make you a life-giver to everyone around, including those who deserve it the least. After all, you didn't deserve it. Charles Spurgeon, a preacher about 150 years ago, showed us who Jesus really is:

"Come unto me," says he, "and I will give you rest." That is the gospel. "I will give you." You say, "Lord, I cannot give you anything." He does not want anything. Come to Jesus, and he says, "I will give you." Not what you give to God but what he gives to you will be your salvation. "I will give you"—that is the gospel in four words. Will you come and have it? It lies open before you.[7]

Jesus the life-giver is the only peace in our tense, life-taking world. He is *your* only peace. Will you receive him today?

4

A Storm Is Coming

PROVERBS 1:20–33

"How long, O simple ones, will you love being simple?"

1:22

WISDOM IS NOT HANDY TIPS to improve our lives like a software upgrade. Wisdom is not a high-octane added ingredient to boost our performance. Wisdom is a matter of life and death, because wisdom reveals we are listening to God with an eager heart. An old hymn helps us hear the gospel clearly:

> Wealth and honor I disdain; earthly comforts, Lord, are vain;
> These can never satisfy; give me Christ, or else I die.

Jesus Christ is not a garnish on the side. Nobody says, "Give me parsley or else I die." The Bible says, "The complacency of fools destroys them; but whoever listens to [Christ] will dwell secure" (Proverbs 1:32, 33).

Chapters 1—9 of Proverbs burn with urgency. We feel it in Proverbs 1:20–33. This passage speaks to us when we slip into the complacency that says, "Sure, I wouldn't mind my life getting a little better." The Bible is saying, "That attitude will destroy you. Now is the time for you to turn a corner!" The famous lyric by Isaac Watts awakens us again to Christ: "Love so amazing, so divine, demands my soul, my life, my all." This passage breaks down into three sections: wisdom is demanding (vv. 20, 21), wisdom is dangerous (vv. 22–31), and wisdom is our only safety (vv. 32, 33).

Wisdom Is Demanding

> Wisdom cries aloud in the street,
>   in the markets she raises her voice;
> at the head of the noisy streets she cries out;
>   at the entrance of the city gates she speaks. (1:20, 21)

In Proverbs 1:8–19 we overheard a father speaking to his son. The book of Proverbs is generally like that—a father-figure preparing his son for true greatness. Now the father points to wisdom as the speaker, wisdom personified as a woman, but not a typical woman, especially for this culture. Women were not given the same voice as men. But Lady Wisdom is standing here at the crossroads of culture—where business, government, education, the arts, athletics all intersect—right in the middle of all the bustle and noise and competition, and she stands up and shouts more loudly than all else. Here is Lady Wisdom the street preacher, warning and scolding and demanding, very unladylike.

Why does Wisdom go out to the streets and markets and city gates? Because the people are there. That is where they live, and where they need wisdom. God's wisdom is not designed for a secluded life. The Beatles in 1966 did not need to fly to India to sit at the feet of the Maharishi. God was trying to get through to them back in Liverpool. And God is speaking to the influencers of our day in London and New York and Nashville. God wants to speak into *your* life with a helpfulness only he can give. We should not think, "When I can thin out my schedule, I might be free to pay more attention." God is free right now, for all that God is.

> Unbelief says: Some other time, but not now; some other place, but not here; some other people, but not us. Faith says: Anything He did anywhere else He will do here; anything He did any other time He is willing to do now; anything He ever did for other people He is willing to do for us! . . . God wants to work through you![1]

God isn't holding out. He is available. But he demands a hearing above all the noise that wants to drown him out.

Wisdom Is Dangerous

> "How long, O simple ones, will you love being simple?
> How long will scoffers delight in their scoffing
>   and fools hate knowledge?
> If you turn at my reproof,
> behold, I will pour out my spirit to you;
>   I will make my words known to you.

Because I have called and you refused to listen,
    have stretched out my hand and no one has heeded,
because you have ignored all my counsel
    and would have none of my reproof,
I also will laugh at your calamity;
    I will mock when terror strikes you,
when terror strikes you like a storm
    and your calamity comes like a whirlwind,
    when distress and anguish come upon you.
Then they will call upon me, but I will not answer;
    they will seek me diligently but will not find me.
Because they hated knowledge
    and did not choose the fear of the LORD,
would have none of my counsel
    and despised all my reproof,
therefore they shall eat the fruit of their way,
    and have their fill of their own devices." (1:22–31)

I say that wisdom is dangerous. But there are two kinds of danger—the danger of poison and the danger of fire. Poison can only be life-threatening. Fire can be helpful. For example, dig some gold ore out of the ground, and it comes up mixed with rock and baser metals. You then smelt it to 80 percent purity. You then refine it in the fire to 99 percent purity, the international gold standard. It takes a metric ton of ore, most of it gunk, to yield about six grams of gold. So much has to be burned away. But the fire does not harm the gold, only the impurities.

Jesus and his wisdom are dangerous like fire. It is our own folly that is dangerous like poison. That is why Wisdom says here in verse 22—we hear the urgency in her tone of voice—"How long, O simple ones, will you love being simple?" We do not have to tell ourselves "I hate wisdom" to miss out on it. We only have to be okay with the way we are. The "scoffers" and "fools," in the rest of verse 22, are more advanced cases, more hardened. A scoffer is an aggressive, confident, calculating person, outwardly impressive, often successful, but he will slit your throat. A fool is a thickheaded, stubborn dolt. He doesn't listen. He always knows better, always has an excuse. Nothing is ever his fault. Both the scoffer and the fool are headed for disaster. But the "simple"—they are the undercommitted, they don't really know what they're living for, they tend to go with the flow and conform—the simple still have a chance. They might respond to Lady Wisdom. That's why she is calling to them. But they need to make up their minds. The problem is, they just don't feel strongly either way. They do not live with urgency. When Lady Wisdom cries out, "How long?" she is saying, "How many sermons is it going to take before you start down a new path?" I heard Peggy Noonan describe one of our former Presidents as "a profoundly unserious person." Christ loves people like that. He is calling to people like that. He takes us seriously. He is calling us to take him seriously and change. Here is what he promises:

"If you turn at my reproof,
behold, I will pour out my spirit to you;
    I will make my words known to you." (Proverbs 1:23)

The Lord is saying, "Sometimes I'll disagree with you, I'll correct you, I'll rebuke you. I don't work with perfect people. I work with responsive people. Here is the response I'm looking for: *turn*." That word "turn" is the most important word in the Bible for repentance. It is not a sentimental word. It is a decisive word. If we decide to turn away from our present selves, both our failures and our attainments, and turn toward Jesus and say to him, "I want you to renew me. If need be, let's go all the way back to John 3:16 and start again. But I am open to you challenging anything in my life. I'm not protecting anything from you. I want to become wise, like you"—if we will turn decisively to him with that openness, what does he promise to do for us?

"I will pour out my spirit to you; I will make my words known to you." What a wonderful assurance. We are all weak, we have tried before, and we are all so tired of failing. We may be thinking, *I do want to turn to him. But how could I keep it up?* Jesus is promising to responsive people, "Batteries are included. I'm wise enough to know all your need. I died to take away your guilt. I rose again to give you my power. I have thought of everything. Trust me and turn." He is promising you, if you turn to him, new passion to sustain you and new insight to intrigue you. He will make the Bible come alive to you. Would you like that? You must decide. Jesus said, "Behold, I stand at the door and knock" (Revelation 3:20). At some point, maybe today, he will knock for the last time, and then silence. What happens then?

Because I have called and you refused to listen . . .
I also will laugh at your calamity. (Proverbs 1:24–26)

If we are too busy for God, he will judge us, and he will not apologize. Hell will never veto the joy of Heaven. God's laughter here is not giggly. He does not laugh at the pain of fools, but he does rejoice at the defeat of evil. So do we: "The whole city celebrates when the godly succeed; they shout for joy when the wicked die" (Proverbs 11:10, NLT). Not only that, but God also laughs in amazement at the stupidity of fools. It's like, "I'm offering you everything you desire in your deepest heart, and you go on marginalizing me? You must be joking." Anything is better than that rebuke from God! That is why it's a mercy when we suffer. Suffering is how our hearts finally crack open to God. It's when we finally stop laughing at *him*. Regina Spektor sings:

> No one laughs at God in a hospital
> No one laughs at God in a war
> No one's laughing at God
> When they're starving or freezing or so very poor
>
> No one laughs at God
> When the doctor calls after some routine tests
> No one's laughing at God
> When it's gotten real late
> And their kid's not back from the party yet
>
> No one laughs at God
> When their airplane starts to uncontrollably shake
> No one's laughing at God
> When they see the one they love hand in hand with someone else
> And they hope that they're mistaken
>
> No one laughs at God
> When the cops knock on their door
> And they say we got some bad news, sir
> No one's laughing at God
> When there's a famine or fire or flood
>
> No one laughs at God on the day they realize
> That the last sight they'll ever see is a pair of hateful eyes
> No one's laughing at God when they're saying their goodbyes[2]

Right now is your moment to turn to God and say, "I am not laughing at you. I am listening to you, whatever you have to say to me." If you are in earnest with God, he will make every promise true for you. But if you turn away, the Bible says a storm is coming: ". . . when terror strikes you like a storm" (v. 27). You know the perfect storm? Not when you fail, but when you succeed and you finally get your perfect life, with you at the center. It's the poison of *your* kingdom coming and *your* will being done. Cynthia Heimel wrote:

> I pity [celebrities]. No, I do. The minute a person becomes a celebrity
> is the same minute he/she becomes a monster. Sylvester Stallone, Bruce
> Willis and Barbra Streisand were once perfectly pleasant human beings

with whom you might lunch on a slow Tuesday afternoon. But now they have become supreme beings, and their wrath is awful. It's not what they had in mind. . . .

The night each of them became famous they wanted to shriek with re-lief. Finally! Now they were adored! Invincible! Magic! The morning after the night each of them became famous, they wanted to take an overdose of barbiturates.

All their fantasies had been realized, yet the reality was still the same. If they were miserable before, they were twice as miserable now, because that giant thing they were striving for, that fame thing that was going to make everything okay, that was going to make their lives bearable, that was going to provide them with personal fulfillment and (ha ha) happiness, had happened. And nothing changed. They were still them. The disillusionment turned them howling and insufferable.[3]

The storm of your life might be when you get what you want, or it might be when your dream dies. Either way, God does not hit you over the head with a hammer. He doesn't have to. The sorrow comes from within the dark energy of your own choices:

They shall eat the fruit of their own way,
    and have their fill of their own devices. (Proverbs 1:31)

God uses no trickery. Hardness of heart inherits itself, and Hell cannot be more inescapable and just than that. C. S. Lewis wrote, "There are only two kinds of people in the end: those who say to God, 'Thy will be done,' and those to whom God says, "Thy will be done.""[4]

Wisdom is dangerous, like fire. But it will purify you. Folly is more dan-gerous, like poison. It will turn you howling and insufferable. *Which danger will you risk?*

I have a friend in California named Ted. He was one of the first hippies back in the mid-1960s. He was a sailmaker in Sausalito, across the bay from San Francisco, when he became a Christian. In a sermon at the church where we both served several years later he said:

You cannot sin and not suffer from it. It just can't be done. I spent a great deal of my life trying to sin and to do away with my conscience at the same time. One of the things I like best about being a Christian is the way that I suffer when I sin—it is the chastisement which guarantees me that I am one of God's people. I like it. It feels good. It feels like correction. It feels as if I am being straightened out. . . . When I was only half-believing God, he actually did come into me and make me miserable every time I sinned. That is how I learned that he really is believable. . . . It corrects me and puts me on the right path.[5]

There is the purifying fire. Is it so bad? It is the love of God getting real with us. Let's receive it.

Wisdom Is Our Only Safety

For the simple are killed by their turning away,
    and the complacency of fools destroys them;
but whoever listens to me will dwell secure
    and will be at ease, without dread of disaster. (Proverbs 1:32, 33)

Note the contrast between the "complacency" of fools in verse 32 and the "ease" of the wise in verse 33. Complacency is counterfeit ease. The truth is, Jesus Christ is dangerous, but he is also the easiest person in the universe to get along with. He said, "My yoke is easy" (Matthew 11:30). He is easier on you than you are on you. He will love you tenderly, correct you helpfully, and carry you faithfully all the way into wisdom forever. And the price you pay for his true ease? "Whoever *listens* to me . . . " Reverent listening sets you apart to Christ, where alone you are safe.

The Bible says, "If you think you are wise . . . you need to become a fool to be truly wise" (1 Corinthians 3:18, NLT). Here is why the Bible says that. You and I both know that this listening to Christ is not easy. We like the word *whoever* in "whoever listens to me will dwell secure" (v. 33). *Everyone* qualifies. There is room for you and me inside that word *whoever*. But the *listens to me* part can be hard. If we listen to Christ, we will change. And we will look stupid in the world's eyes for the rest of our lives. Are you willing? The world offers complacency. That is its false promise. Christ offers you ease. That is his true promise to all who listen to him with urgency. What is your next step of obedience to the Lord Jesus? It might be scary. But not taking that step is even more scary.

Jesus took these words from Wisdom personified into his own mouth as Wisdom incarnate. He too warned of a storm coming. He told us that everyone who hears him and obeys him will be like a wise man who builds his house on a rock (Matthew 7:24–27). When the storm comes, it doesn't matter, because the rock of grace will hold. But everyone who does not listen will be like a foolish man who builds his life on sand—the sand of "Don't rush me," "I'm not that bad," "I'm too busy right now," "Maybe later"—the constantly shifting sand of Self. And when the storm comes, that house falls, and catastrophic is its fall.

5

How We Can Grow

PROVERBS 2:1–22

. . . wisdom will come into your heart.

2:10

PROVERBS 2 OPENS A DOOR TO EVERY ONE OF US. We all want to grow in Christ. In this passage God is telling us *how* we can move forward. If you see a sign in front of a church, "Revival here next week," you can be sure there won't be a revival there next week. We do not program God or control God. But in this passage God himself tells us how to take our next steps into newness of life. We want to change. We want to get closer to him, closer than we have ever gone before, closer than we have ever dreamed of going. Now God is telling us *how*.

We feel disqualified, and we are. But that is not a deal-breaker for God. With him, there is only one deal-breaker: "The *complacency* of fools destroys them" (Proverbs 1:32). You do not need to hate Jesus to waste your life. You only need to be okay with how you are. But if your heart is lonely for God and longing for a better life, can't you see here in verses 1–4 that anyone can go deep with God, anyone with a heart for God?

Proverbs 2 is one of the most helpful passages in the Bible, because it explains what growth and sanctification and renewal—what all of that *feels* like. This passage explains the psychology of change. This new mentality is the opposite of complacency. What happens inside people who are seeing God in powerful new ways? Is my soul in that positive condition today? Is yours? Can we go there together? God has brought us to this passage to open that door for every one of us.

The flow of thought in Proverbs 2 is clear. The structure can be outlined in this simple, twofold way:

1. You can be renewed in God (vv. 1–11)
    A. Get real with God (vv. 1–4)
    B. And God will get real with you (vv. 5–8)
    C. And you will change (vv. 9–11)

2. You can be protected in this world (vv. 12–22)
    A. Safe from devious men (vv. 12–15)
    B. Safe from deadly women (vv. 16–19)
    C. Safe forever in God's place of blessing (vv. 20–22)

You do not need to run from life. You only need to run toward God, and he will prepare you for real life.

You Can Be Renewed in God

Verses 1–4 tell us how to get real with God. If these verses describe how you feel about him, you can thank him, because he is already at work in your heart. No matter who you are or what you have done, here is the non-complacency that the grace of God stirs up within us:

> My son, if you receive my words
>   and treasure up my commandments with you,
> making your ear attentive to wisdom
>   and inclining your heart to understanding;
> yes, if you call out for insight
>   and raise your voice for understanding,
> if you seek it like silver
>   and search for it as for hidden treasures . . . (Proverbs 2:1–4)

We see the word "if" in verse 1, again in verse 3, and again in verse 4. We also see the word "then" in verse 5 and again in verse 9. Those are the markers of verses 1–11 that map out the process of change: "If . . . then . . . " Now, some of us may be thinking, "Wait a minute. That sounds like legalism. How can the grace of God be conditional?" How can the grace of God *not* be conditional? We cannot deserve his grace or earn it. But we must reach for it decisively, allowing nothing to stand in our way.

Think of it like this. You and I are standing on the brink of the Grand Canyon in Arizona. It is magnificent. You are loving what your eyes have the privilege of seeing. I am standing there beside you. My eyesight is bad, so I put on my glasses. But the lenses are dirty and smudgy and scratched and filthy. I cannot enter into all that magnificence right in front of me. So you say, "Ray, clean your glasses." And I say to you, "Now don't get legalistic on me!" You are not being legalistic. Legalism is thinking I can do something to make God pay attention to me. Legalism is thinking I can do something to deserve the grace of God. Legalism is *meritorious* thinking. But this passage is simply asking every one of us, are you paying attention?

How does God want us to pay attention to him? As his beloved children, already accepted in Christ. Verse 1 begins, "My son . . . " We don't earn that place in God's heart. He gives it freely through Christ. It is his fatherly love that speaks to us here, calling us to take new steps of growth toward him. Those new steps of stretching and seeking are found in the verbs. Look at the verbs in verses 1–4. Look how they escalate in intensity: "If you receive . . . treasure up . . . making your ear attentive . . . inclining your heart . . . call out . . . raise your voice . . . seek . . . search . . . " Do you see the point? Wisdom is not automatic for us. Wisdom is not our default setting. We will never get there by drifting. You cannot become a significant person by being neutral and cute and safely unchanged. That is complacency. God is offering you a treasure infinitely worth seeking—more of himself entering into you, renewing you, safeguarding you. I do not know what your most personal need is today. But I do know this: God is saying to you, "My child, I am so available—*if* you want me more than you want your own status quo." Will you give yourself completely to God today? Will you say to him right now, "I want to change more than I want to stay the way I am. I am now *hurling myself* into your arms"? That is the wholeheartedness God requires. C. S. Lewis explained why:

> God cannot bless us, unless he has us. When we try to keep within us an area that is our own, we try to keep an area of death. Therefore, in love, God claims all. There's no bargaining with him.[1]

The status quo you are afraid to let go of—why is that so great? Who is telling you that God is a bad risk? Who is telling you that you are okay the way you are? Is God your Father saying that to you? I read this comment on a recent blog post:

> I live in an upper-class suburb surrounded by a great deal of kind, responsible religious people who find great encouragement in people like Joel Osteen and Oprah. They speak often of "God's potential" for their lives, and often relate the gospel with self-made material success.
>
> Many of them attend my Episcopal church and at times I have found myself sitting in the pews thinking, "The words in this Prayer Book about sin, sickness, powerlessness, death, propitiation, justification, and resurrection don't make any sense at all [to these people]. . . . They're not perfect, but they're doing just fine."

But then a few days later I spend time with their kids and realize that they have parents who are dying, who are unflinchingly racist, who are openly cheating one another, and who are addicted to alcohol and/or cocaine. And that's just the obvious stuff. But everyone comes to church with smiling faces. It's weird, you know?

One of the most common teachings I've heard from [Oprah and Osteen] regarding success in life is, "You've got to stop spending time with those people who are holding you back, the kind of people who are always stuck in a rut. They're going to drag you down with them."

Why do we buy into that? People long for love, not success. When was the last time you saw a feel-good movie that ended with, "And then she ditched all her friends so she could finally get that position at Bank of America"? Movies resolve with love because people long for love, even if they get dragged down with the beloved in the end (which they almost certainly will).[2]

God our Father loved us enough for his only Son to get dragged down at the cross for us. Here is how we respond to his love. We turn from our complacent wonderfulness, and we turn back to God through the urgency of prayer, confession, repentance, and seeking. There is no set of rules to tell us what to do here in verses 1–4. It's all about *desire* for God.

What does God promise to those who seek him with an openness to change? Here is what every true seeker can count on from God:

then you will understand the fear of the LORD
    and find the knowledge of God.
For the LORD gives wisdom;
    from his mouth come knowledge and understanding;
he stores up sound wisdom for the upright;
    he is a shield to those who walk in integrity,
guarding the paths of justice
    and watching over the way of his saints. (Proverbs 2:5–8)

God is not saying, "If you seek me, I will love you more." He is saying, "If you seek me, you will find me, for all that I am worth." You can know God, personally, in ways that will help you and guard you. How does this miracle enter into our experience? Verse 6 says: ". . . from his mouth come knowledge and understanding." The Bible is the mouth of God today—not a voice speaking within our minds but the Bible lying open before our eyes. On my seventeenth birthday my dad and mom gave me a new Bible. This is what dad wrote inside:

Bud, nothing could be greater than to have a son—a son who loves the Lord and walks with him. Your mother and I have found this Book our dearest treasure. We give it to you and doing so can give nothing greater. Be a student of the Bible and your life will be full of blessing. We love you. Dad

Our heavenly Father is promising that to all of us in verses 5–8. We do not have to be geniuses. We only have to be straight with him: "He stores up sound wisdom *for the upright*" (v. 7). If we will seek God honestly, he will deal with us directly.

What else can we count on from God if we see him as verses 1–4 urge us to? We notice another "Then" at the beginning of verse 9, followed by more assurances:

Then you will understand righteousness and justice
    and equity, every good path;
for wisdom will come into your heart,
    and knowledge will be pleasant to your soul;
discretion will watch over you,
    understanding will guard you. (Proverbs 2:9–11)

God is able to give your heart a new taste, a new relish, a new instinct for wisdom. If you want to be a better husband, if you want to get out of credit card debt, if you want to know how much TV to watch (or not watch), you do not need someone to beat you down with guilt and pressure. You do not need five easy steps to this or seven sure-fire principles for that. You need a new heart, new character, an awakening deep within. And God is saying, "If you will seek me, wisdom will come into your heart, and knowledge will be pleasant to your soul." Wise people do not pout and whine, "Do I *have* to?" Their hearts are set free: "You mean I *get* to?" They *love* the things of God as satisfying to the appetites of their renewed souls. They experience what Jesus said: "Blessed are those who hunger and thirst for righteousness, for they shall be satisfied" (Matthew 5:6).

Our Father is saying in Proverbs 2, "If you will seek newness of life in Christ (vv. 1–4), you will go deep with him (vv. 5–8), and you will change within yourself (vv. 9–11). Then you'll be prepared for life in the real world (vv. 12–22)." That is *how* grace works.

You Can Be Protected in This World

With God's wisdom soaking down into our hearts, we are fortified against two temptations that we inevitably face in this world. The first temptation is described in verses 12–15:

> . . . delivering you from the way of evil,
>   from men of perverted speech,
> who forsake the paths of uprightness
>   to walk in the ways of darkness,
> who rejoice in doing evil
>   and delight in the perverseness of evil,
> men whose paths are crooked,
>   and who are devious in their ways. (Proverbs 2:12–15)

The key is in verse 12: "men of perverted speech." They are often highly impressive, successful, formidable men. You secretly hope that they will include you in their "inner ring" at the office or the dorm or the recording studio.[3] Over coffee one day in friendly conversation, the hint will come that they want you, they are welcoming you in. It will mean a little bending of the rules now and then, but cool people are never held back by that. In your insecurity you want to be included. But if you take that step, the next time you will go further away from Christ, and the next time further still. You might end up in scandal and even prison, or you might end up on top of the heap. But either way you will be a fool, with a heart that loves darkness.

Here is what you need to know, so that your heart can stay on alert as you move among such men this week. "Perverted speech" is not limited to bad words and dirty jokes. It includes even good words, but good words being used to turn things upside down. Upheaval, turning things upside down and inside out—that is the force of the Hebrew behind the word "perverted." Words should represent reality, they should be true to what is; but words can be used to twist reality, words can be used to flip meanings into their opposite. In politics, for example, listen for the way people use a good word like *patriotism*. In sociology, listen for the way people use a good word like *family*. In religion, listen for the way people use a good word like *Jesus*. Bad men use good words to smuggle in bad realities, and some people are fooled. But if wisdom has entered your heart, tricky words just won't pass the whiff test. You might not be able to explain what bothers you, but you will be protected by the wisdom God has put inside you.

The God-given wisdom deep in your heart will also protect you from a second temptation, described in verses 16–19:

> So you will be delivered from the forbidden woman,
>   from the adulteress with her smooth words,
> who forsakes the companion of her youth
>   and forgets the covenant of her God;
> for her house sinks down to death,

and her paths to the departed;
none who go to her come back
    nor do they regain the paths of life. (Proverbs 2:16–19)

The key here is in verse 16: "her smooth words." Again, words are what we must watch for. When a married woman says to another man, "I want you, you're handsome, you make me feel alive again"—that woman has forsaken the man she fell in love with and has forgotten her covenant with Christ (v. 17). This is a churchgoing woman in view here. And *she* is offering you her love? Her husband means nothing to her, and she wants *you* involved? Verses 18, 19 are warning us that there is no such thing as a one-night stand. It isn't that simple. It gets complicated fast. We need nothing less than an almighty Savior to extricate us from the bondage of sexual sin. Thank God for Jesus! But if wisdom has entered your heart, you will know what to do, right then and there, at the moment of temptation. Run! If you are married, go home to your wife, look deeply into her eyes, tell her you love her, and give your heart to her completely, for the sheer joy of it, all over again. If you are single, go home, kneel down in prayer, and give yourself, body and soul, all over again to your Savior and Lord. That is wisdom going down deep, protecting you.

But wisdom is more than avoiding sin. That would be merely negative. Wisdom also escorts us into the path of everything desirable:

So you will walk in the way of the good
    and keep to the paths of the righteous.
For the upright will inhabit the land,
    and those with integrity will remain in it,
but the wicked will be cut off from the land,
    and the treacherous will be rooted out of it. (Proverbs 2:20–22)

Here in the conclusion to Proverbs 2, the father-figure points to the resource we all need for constant new beginnings in our lives. The Bible is not holding up a standard and leaving us to ourselves. These verses are good news for weak people. The clue is "the land," the place of God's blessing, in verses 21, 22. If you want a new heart of wisdom, you've got company— "the good," "the righteous," "the upright," and "those with integrity." But far better, we are all together in "the land"—that is, in New Testament terms, in Christ. "Inhabiting the land" is Old Testament code language for "abiding in Christ." Jesus said, "If you abide in me, and my words abide in you, ask whatever you wish, and it will be done for you" (John 15:7). What will you ask your all-sufficient Savior to do for you today, as you in your weakness face the temptations of this world?

Your most meaningful prayer is to "call out for insight" and "raise your voice for understanding" (v. 3). The whole passage is meant to position us in that place of blessing and protection. We need it. A tsunami of sin is slamming us in our world today, and all of us are suffering under it. Sometimes that suffering is our own fault, because we have been complacent and unguarded. Other times that suffering is precisely because we have stayed true to the Lord. However we are suffering, our real business is with Christ. He is saying to us here in his Word, "Come to me. Deal with me. I am able to restore you out of your past failings and defend you for the future. Hurl yourself at me in all your need. I will give myself to you in all my grace. My wisdom will enter your heart in ways you've never known before."

Will you come to Christ today?

6

The Wisdom That *Helps* Us

PROVERBS 3:1–8

Trust in the LORD with all your heart.

3:5

WHY ARE WE STUDYING THE BOOK OF PROVERBS? Because we need more than ethical principles. We need new hearts. We need wisdom deep within, at an intuitive level, as we hurry from one complex decision to the next, moment by moment, in the concrete realities of our daily lives. Without God's wisdom, many difficulties in life will remain confusing and threatening. With God's wisdom entering our hearts, we get the hang of how life really works, and we come alive more and more. Irenaeus, the early Christian theologian, famously said, "The glory of God is man fully alive."[1] That is where Proverbs 3 wants to take us.

The wisdom of Proverbs 2 offered to deliver us from evil. It offered protection. But this glowing chapter 3 is so positive. It is an education in life at its best—how to live well in every area, at home, at work, all around. In Proverbs 3:1–8, God is showing us the way into *shalom* (v. 2), "good success" (v. 4), and "refreshment" (v. 8). This is not a matter of earning God's love. As in Proverbs 2, the passage begins with "My son" in verse 1. God is speaking to us as his beloved ones, his adopted children. He was not stuck with us. He chose us, because he loves us, and now he is coaching us in how we can be fully alive, for his glory.

But there is a problem here. Let's address it up front. The wise father-figure offers us "length of days and years of life" (v. 2), "favor and good success" (v. 4), "barns . . . filled with plenty [and] vats . . . bursting with wine" (v. 10), and "riches and honor" (v. 16). Is this the prosperity gospel? You know what I mean—the idea that God is out to make you healthy and rich and comfortable and put you on top of the heap because you are his child. Is this passage saying that? Can we trust this counsel? Can we swallow it whole? I offer two answers.

First, the prosperity gospel is found *nowhere* in the Bible. The prosperity gospel is coldhearted materialism in religious disguise. It chooses Bible verses selectively to fit a name-it-and-claim-it theory, but it does not love God. It wants to use God for selfish, infantile purposes. Where does the prosperity gospel say, as the gospel clearly says in Philippians 3:7–11 (I will paraphrase it), "I have lost everything, and I'm cool with that, because I've gained Christ. I have been stripped bare. I have nothing left. All I have is Christ, and I'm happy, because he loves me, and that satisfies my heart"? *That* is the gospel, and *that* is true prosperity.

Second, the rewards God offers us here in Proverbs 3 are good. He will give them out to his wise children, as he sees fit. But every believer's life is complicated. God sends us pain too. Verses 11, 12 are clear that God disciplines us. God sends both earthly blessings and earthly sorrows. Think of Jesus. He both suffered at the cross and prospered in the resurrection. And the resurrection is the prosperity you will want when your health utterly fails, as it will, and very soon. If your story is limited to the blessings of the here and now, you are in trouble, because your vats bursting with wine will also run dry. But if your life in this world is only the title page to your eternal story, and God also gives you some barns and vats for the present, okay. Just be sure you set your heart not on the gift, which will certainly fail you, but on the Giver, who will certainly never fail you. C. S. Lewis counseled us wisely:

> The settled happiness and security which we all desire, God withholds from us by the very nature of the world; but joy, pleasure and merriment he has scattered broadcast. We are never safe, but we have plenty of fun, and some ecstasy. It is not hard to see why. The security we all crave would teach us to rest our hearts in this world and oppose an obstacle to our return to God; a few moments of happy love, a landscape, a symphony, a merry meeting with our friends, a bath or a football match, have no such tendency. Our Father refreshes us on the journey with some pleasant inns, but will not encourage us to mistake them for home.[2]

The passage is organized around two themes: the *shalom* God gives (vv. 1–4) and the trust God demands (vv. 5–8). That is obvious. But look more closely. Do you see how the wise Father links his *counsel* with *incentives* all along the way? For example, in verses 1, 2,

> *Counsel:* My son, do not forget my teaching,
>   but let your heart keep my commandments,
> *Incentive:* for length of days and years of life
>   and peace they will add to you.

Step by step, the father gives his counsel and then adds an incentive. He is not saying, "Do this because I say so." He is saying, "Do this because it will help you." This is the gospel for sinners whom God treats as his own dear children, guiding us, counseling us, urging us on, blessing us. How does he want to help us?

The *Shalom* God Gives

> My son, do not forget my teaching,
>   but let your heart keep my commandments,
> for length of days and years of life
>   and peace they will add to you. (Proverbs 3:1, 2)

What is the Father saying? "Pay attention. Pay attention to *me*. You're going to pay attention to something. But only my teaching will lead you into *shalom*, wholeness, peace." God is not saying we have to be smart. In fact, if we are wise in our own eyes, that is a problem (v. 7). It is okay to be incompetent. But we do have to pay attention to his gospel and its implications—his teaching and his commandments.

In all the noise of our culture, what are you listening to? And is it working for you? Or is it a mirage, leading you on with false promises, always just out of reach? Mark Rutherford, in his novel *The Revolution in Tanner's Lane*, says: "If your religion doesn't help you, it is no religion for you; you had better be without it."[3] Whatever you are paying attention to—is it leading you into peace? Be honest about that. If it is not helping you, there is a reason. Look more closely at that. Drill down there. Is it the Father's teaching you are paying attention to, or are you paying more attention to some popular but defunct theory that cannot possibly work out?

In the second line of verse 1, the word "keep" means more than "obey"; it means "guard, maintain vigilance." "Let your heart *guard* my commandments." Your heart is your security system. And every day thieves are trying to rob you of length of days and years of life and peace. Elsewhere the Bible calls them "idols." What are they? Just obsolete ideas that cannot help because they are made up. Our own hearts produce them. For example, ask yourself, "What life scenario will make me say, 'I have finally arrived'? What does 'arrival' look like to me?" Whatever that scenario is, if Christ is not the life-giving center, your heart has already been penetrated by a life-robbing idol. There is a reason why the sage is telling us to stay alert. When we forget Christ, we are not released into freedom; we submit to false teachings that fill our lives with regret. For example, if you feel that you will finally "arrive" through your career, then you can never relax, because you are literally working for your salvation. If you believe your family will "make" your existence, your "arrival" is insecure, because your kids will break your heart. However you define your *shalom*, if it is not Christ, then it is an idol, demanding your all but giving nothing. If you obey it, it will break its promises. If you fail to obey it, it will punish you. Here is the point. Our problem is not just our wandering wills; our problem is our false beliefs. Our minds give credit to lies. That is why our Father is saying, "Stay alert to what you're believing moment by moment. My teaching alone can make you lie down in green pastures and beside still waters. Pay attention to the gospel of the finished work of Christ for sinners. If you'll guard my teaching with your heart, you will experience it as your true *shalom*."

> Let not steadfast love and faithfulness forsake you;
>> bind them around your neck;
>> write them on the tablet of your heart.
> So you will find favor and good success
>> in the sight of God and man. (Proverbs 3.3, 4)

The key here is "steadfast love and faithfulness." Those words describe God himself (Exodus 34:6). What are we counting on about God? We are staking everything on God's being steadfastly loving and faithful to us forever through Christ, because he promised to be. The sage is saying to us, "You know that's who God is. He told you so in the Bible. Okay, let who God is change you." So much American religion is not about who God is. So much American religion makes us the immovable ones, the center around which God orbits. American religion is not about us changing and repenting and adjusting to who God is. It is about God making us feel better about ourselves without our having to change. But the truth is, God is who he is, so that we can become more like him. And after all, isn't that what we want? A person of steadfast love and faithfulness can be trusted. You have nothing to fear from such a person. You have everything to admire in such a person. God is in that person. And he wants to make you more like himself.

So many people have been let down by Christians. They do not believe anymore, because they did not see the reality of God in God's people. They saw people wearing crosses around their necks but without binding steadfast love and faithfulness around their necks. The fraudulence of that makes people angry. And they have a right to be angry. So the Father is saying here to his children, "My steadfast love and faithfulness to sinners—let that be your persona. Wear that reality in public, because it's who Jesus is. I want you to be like him right out in the open, for other sinners to see and have hope." When people see Jesus in us, we find favor and good success. There is no other way. We would not want it any other way.

That then is the *shalom* God gives. It is both personal (vv. 1, 2) and social (vv. 3, 4). How do we get there? Here is how:

The Trust God Demands

> Trust in the LORD with all your heart,
>   and do not lean on your own understanding.
> In all your ways acknowledge him,
>   and he will make straight your paths. (Proverbs 3:5, 6)

These are the most famous verses in Proverbs. What are they saying? They are saying that our confidence is not some impersonal ethic but the Lord Jesus Christ himself. And the kind of trust he deserves and demands is wholehearted trust: "Trust in the LORD *with all your heart*." One of my seminary professors told about his father crossing the Susquehanna River one winter's day. His dad did not know how thick the ice was. So he was crawling along on all fours, gingerly feeling his way forward, when he heard some racket and clatter coming up behind him. He looked back, and here came a wagon pulled by four horses, and the driver was whipping them along at a pretty good clip right across the frozen river. The guy was a local. He knew how thick the ice was. Too many Christians are like the man down on all fours, creeping along, way too cautious. Their trust in the Lord is halfhearted. Then along comes a wholehearted Christian, and he changes the tone for everyone around.

This Hebrew verb translated "trust" is cognate with an Arabic verb that means to throw oneself down on one's face, to lie down spread-eagle in complete reliance—to make it as graphic as I can, to do a belly-flop on God with all our sin and all our failure and all our fears. We stake everything on the gospel promises of God. If God fails us, we are damned. If God comes through, we are saved forever. Real trust is that blunt and daring and simple. A. W. Tozer nailed it:

Pseudo-faith always arranges a way out to serve in case God fails it. Real faith knows only one way and gladly allows itself to be stripped of any second way or makeshift substitutes. For true faith, it is either God or total collapse. And not since Adam stood up on the earth has God failed a single man or woman who trusted him.[4]

I am calling you today to trust in the Lord Jesus Christ with everything that shames you and terrifies you and holds you back. Let your full weight down on him. He will never fail anyone who trusts him radically. No pseudo-faith, because he's no pseudo-Savior! He is real. He is all he claims to be. He is right now all he has ever been to anyone anywhere. And he offers his total Self to you today on terms of total grace. What he deserves and demands is your total trust in the love and mercy and wisdom of God in Christ alone.

But how can you tell if your trust is wholehearted? None of us wants to be halfhearted. You men, when you were ten years old and someone asked you what you wanted to be when you grew up, not one of you said, "When I grow up, I want to be wishy-washy!" You said something like, "I want to be a Green Beret!" or "I want to be a fighter pilot!" And now today we want to be all-out for Christ. So let's examine ourselves. Here are three diagnostics for wholehearted trust in the Lord.

First, do you let the Bible overrule your own thinking? It says in verse 5, "Do not lean on your own understanding." Do you merely agree with the Bible, or do you obey the Bible? My dog sometimes agrees with me, but she never obeys me. If you merely agree with the Bible, then your response is not obedience but coincidence. It's just that the prejudices you have soaked up from your culture happen to line up with the Bible at that point. But what do you do when the Bible contradicts what you want to be true? If you are looking in the Bible for excuses to do what you want anyway, you have in fact rejected God. But if you trust the Lord, you will let the Bible challenge your most cherished thoughts and feelings. The wonderful thing is, the Lord cares about your questions and problems. He wants to speak into your life in ways that will help you. If you will trust him wholeheartedly, you will let him teach you.

Second, do you believe someone somewhere without Jesus will still go to Heaven? Do people really need Jesus to have peace with God? Or is it okay with God if they're just sincere, well-meaning people? If you think so, you are probably putting yourself into that scenario, because *you* are not sure about Jesus. You are not trusting Jesus to save you; you are hoping Jesus will flatter you. But if you trust the Lord entirely, you will also trust him exclusively, as your only Savior, as anyone's only Savior.

Third, when was the last time you took a risk to obey Christ? When was the last time you diminished your future—socially, financially, professionally—for his sake? When was the last time your life looked obviously different from the life of someone who does not trust Jesus at all? If you never surprise an unbelieving friend by your sacrifices for Christ, it is probably because what you are living for is the same earthly payoff he is living for. But if you trust the Lord entirely, you will also trust him exhaustively, across the whole of life. You will not be a fragmented person. You will not think piecemeal. You will (verse 6 literally translated) "know him" in all your ways.[5] Then he promises to direct the course of your life straight on to where you want to go. "He will make straight your paths" is a wonderful assurance. If you will let Jesus rule as Lord over the whole of your life, he will so enter into your story and so make straight your paths that all things will work together for your good. Will you trust him with all your heart?

I saw this at my twenty-year high school reunion. I loved high school and had missed my friends over the years. But at the reunion I saw a difference among them. Some had thrown themselves into the craziness of the sixties, and they had aged prematurely. I have to hand it to them. They tried with all their might to have a good time that night. But it seemed forced. I saw other friends who had walked with Christ. I remember one girl in particular. She had been shy back in her teens. But now she was an outgoing, radiant, lovely woman with sparkle and charm. She had trusted the Lord with all her heart, and she was living proof of his wisdom.

Here is the price—if we can call it that—here is the price we pay to walk with God in a way that really helps us:

Be not wise in your own eyes;
    fear the Lord, and turn away from evil.
It will be healing to your flesh
    and refreshment to your bones. (Proverbs 3:7, 8)

The Father is warning us against a spirit of self-assurance. It is the opposite of trust in the Lord, and it brings no healing and refreshment. Maybe you remember Frank Sinatra's old song, "My Way":

And now the end is near, and so I face the final curtain
My friend, I'll say it clear, I'll state my case of which I'm certain
I've lived a life that's full, I traveled each and every highway
And more, much more than this, I did it my way

Yes there were times, I'm sure you knew
When I bit off more than I could chew
But through it all, when there was doubt, I ate it up and spit it out
I faced it all and I stood tall, and did it my way

For what is a man, what has he got?
If not himself, then he has naught
To say the things he truly feels and not the words of one who kneels
The record shows I took the blows, and did it my way.

That's stupid. But it has over three million views on YouTube. We glorify the know-it-all who does it his own way. But the Bible says, "Do you see a man who is wise in his own eyes? There is more hope for a fool than for him" (Proverbs 26:12). A spirit of self-assurance will destroy you and everyone you love. It *cannot* work. The universe will not cooperate with our arrogant self-centeredness. But fearing the Lord and turning away from evil—calling sin sin and turning from it—is healing and refreshment. Notice that. It's not just that you will avoid pain; you will enjoy the positive energy of healing and refreshment. Here is the irony. The more you fear the Lord, the less you will fear man. The more you depend on the Lord, the more independent you will be. The more you resemble Christ, the more an individual you will be. The more you obey him, the freer you will be. Life will work for you with healing and refreshment.

Fear the Lord and turn away from evil. Yes, it's a simple thing to say. But we need to be told, because it is radical. The first of Martin Luther's 95 Theses was this: "Our Lord and Master Jesus Christ, in saying, 'Repent,' intended that the whole life of believers should be repentance." You probably have a to-do list for this coming week. Here are the priorities God wants at the top of your list in terms of urgency. #1: Fear the Lord. #2: Turn away from evil. #3: As time permits, breathe. That is the urgency of your life this week. It will add greatness to your life. It will add life to your life. It will save you from a wasted life. John Wesley, the founder of the Methodist movement, said this:

Give me one hundred preachers who fear nothing but sin and desire nothing but God, and I care not a straw whether they be clergymen or laymen, such alone will shake the gates of hell and set up the kingdom of God upon earth.[6]

If you want your life to count now and forever for Christ, here is all you need to do. *Fear the Lord. Turn away from evil.* Do that alone, and your life will be magnificent.

7

Wisdom at the Extremes of Life

PROVERBS 3:9–12

Honor the LORD with your wealth.

3:9

Do not despise the LORD's discipline.

3:11

HERE WE ARE AT THE TWO OPPOSITE EXTREMES OF LIFE—when the good times roll and when hardship strikes. When life is sweet, trusting God with all our hearts feels unnecessary. When life is bitter, trusting God with all our hearts feels impossible. We need wisdom for those seasons in life when we are on top and for those seasons in life when nothing is going right. God is with us in both, with a wisdom that makes a positive difference. Earlier in Proverbs 3, God calls us to trust him wholeheartedly (v. 5). Now, in Proverbs 3:9–12, he leads us to trust him wholeheartedly when we are pushed out to these two opposite edges of our lives—plenty and pain.

Wisdom in Plenty

> Honor the LORD with your wealth
>   and with the firstfruits of all your produce;
> then your barns will be filled with plenty,
>   and your vats will be bursting with wine. (Proverbs 3:9, 10)

The sage gives us his counsel (v. 9), with an incentive (v. 10). What is

his counsel? "Honor the LORD with your wealth." The Hebrew verb translated "honor" means "to treat the Lord as weighty."[1] The root of the verb
means "to be heavy," even as we today might say that a person carries social
weight. That is what money communicates—prestige, rank, importance. It
is all around us every day. In my part of God's world, the Nashville area
may be one of the most intense concentrations of money in the history of
the human race. Whose prestige is that money enhancing? The sad truth is,
we honor *ourselves* with our money, and the Lord gets second best if he is
lucky. But wisdom changes us. Wisdom is saying, "Make *the Lord* famous
and prominent by means of your wealth. Use your money to increase *his*
prestige in your world."

Why is using our money for Christ wise? Because the more we use our
money for self-importance, the sillier we look. The pretense of it, the love
of appearances, the overreaching—we do that because money has an almost
mystical power over us. But how many castles in Europe are still lived in by
the families that built them? Self-importance is unsustainable. But the more
we heap prestige on Jesus by our money, the more weighty and significant
and relevant *we* become. We become serious people. We impact history. That
is the irony of wisdom.

There is also a Hebrew verb for the opposite of honoring. It means "to
make light of, to regard as trifling and frivolous." As God looks at your financial priorities, should he consider himself honored or slighted? *Somebody*
gets the honor of first place in your monthly budget. Who is in that first place
of honor?

If God grants revival in our time—and we always pray for revival—God
will be restored to his place of honor in every area of our lives. This word
in verse 9 translated "honor" is the Old Testament word for glory. Don't we
pray, "Show us your glory" (see Exodus 33:18)? That is a meaningful prayer.
The glory of God is why you and I are on the planet. The glory of God is why
the planet is here. The glory of God is why everything is here. What is God
up to in all of this? He is displaying his glory, so that we can thrill over him
forever. The glory of God is the central theme of the Bible.[2] Everything that
is wrong with the world today is traceable to this one mega-sin—trivializing
God. And that is folly. Life *cannot* work when we shut out the glory of God
and treat this imposter called Self as weighty. But it is so freeing to throw
ourselves into honoring God with all we have, including our money.

David Wells, in his book *God in the Wasteland*, speaks of "the weight-
lessness of God," meaning that who God is makes little felt difference in
our world today.[3] We Christians want to change that. We reject what Os

Guinness, in his book *The Gravedigger File*, calls "the Cheshire Cat factor." Remember in *Alice in Wonderland* how the Cheshire cat began to vanish from the end of its tail forward, until nothing was left but the grin?[4] We do not want the glory of God to fade away to a stupid grin as we represent him in our time. We grieve when God is removed from the power centers of our culture. We know something is wrong when the founder of McDonald's hamburgers says, "I speak of faith in McDonald's as if it were a religion. I believe in God, family and McDonald's—and in the office that order is reversed."[5] We know that order of priorities dishonors God. But what about us? *Does anything in our financial priorities carry more weight than God?* "Honor the LORD with your wealth."

Here are three things you must understand about verses 9, 10. First, the ESV says, "Honor the LORD *with* your wealth." But the NASB is a more literal translation: "Honor the LORD *from* your wealth." What difference does that make? I might say, "Hey, I'm honoring the Lord when I pay my light bill on time and when I take my wife out to dinner and so forth, because all my money belongs to God and I'm doing good things with it, I'm not doing bad things, and that honors the Lord." That is how I might "honor the Lord" *with* my wealth, and I could do that without ever giving a dime away. But Proverbs 3:9 is actually saying, "Honor the LORD *from* your wealth." That is, he gets a cut from my wealth. I part with some of my money for his sake. I give it away for his sake.

Second, the next line of the verse explains *how* I truly honor the Lord from my wealth: ". . . and with the firstfruits of all your produce." The first-fruits were the best of the harvest (Numbers 18:12, 13). Exodus 23:19 says, "The best of the firstfruits of your ground you shall bring into the house of the LORD your God." So then, how do we honor the Lord from our wealth? By giving away to him *our first and our best*. He comes first in our budgets—ahead even of taxes.

Third, I truly honor the Lord from my wealth when I calculate not from the net but from the gross, because it says, "from *all* your produce," that is, *all* our income. We can dishonor God not only by not giving him anything but also by giving him the leftovers after we have taken care of ourselves in our monthly budgets. Our giving to the Lord can be like a tip thrown on the table. But we honor him by giving to him the first cut *from our gross income*.

How can wise people be tightfisted? God our Father is sharing *his* resources with us to expand the family business—the gospel enterprise. He is entrusting into our care his own money, and we are investing his funds for his greater glory in the world today. He has made us his investment brokers.

We invest 10 percent as a tithe, and he pays us a 90 percent commission! He is such a good boss to work for.

God loves to give even more to his children who understand what money is for and handle it wisely:

> . . . then your barns will be filled with plenty,
>   and your vats will be bursting with wine. (Proverbs 3:10)

God's capacity to give far exceeds our capacity to receive. Jesus said, "Give, and it will be given to you. Good measure, pressed down, shaken together, running over, will be put into your lap. For with the measure you use it will be measured back to you" (Luke 6:38). He does *not* mean by that, "Give money to God, and he'll make you rich." If that were the message, the Lord would not be honored, he would be used. Jesus is not arousing our greed. When then does he mean? He means, as God's people have experienced with great joy throughout history, if you invest for his sake, he will give you more to invest for his sake. Matthew Henry, the old Puritan scholar, said this about verse 10:

> God will bless you with an increase of that which is for use, not for show, for giving away, not for hoarding. Those who do good with what they have shall have more to do more good with.[6]

If you love Jesus, nothing could make you happier than to do more good for his sake. Why? Because here is how he treated you: "For you know the grace of our Lord Jesus Christ, that though he was rich, yet for your sake he became poor, so that you by his poverty might become rich" (2 Corinthians 8:9). Someone like that should be honored, don't you think?

Wisdom in Pain

> My son, do not despise the Lord's discipline
>   or be weary of his reproof,
> for the Lord reproves him whom he loves,
>   as a father the son in whom he delights. (Proverbs 3:11, 12)

This reminds me of The Rolling Stones' song, "There've been good times, there've been bad times, I've had my share of hard times too." The bad times and the hard times seem to double up. When (not if) that happens, honesty forces us to face the only two possibilities about God. Either God loves us passionately, or God hates our guts. It is one or the other. And we all have moments when it feels like God despises us. That is why we are thankful for the opening words in verse 11: "My son . . . " Do you hear the tenderness in those words? A wise father is counseling the son he loves. What is he saying about the hard times? Two things.

First, *when we suffer, it isn't God angrily taking from us; it is God lovingly reinvesting in us.* Suffering feels like anger. It feels like loss. It feels like God has abandoned us. But the heroes of faith in Hebrews 11 suffered. Theirs was no country club religion. They trusted God with all their hearts, and some were tortured, killed, mistreated. Was God mad at them? No; he commended them (Hebrews 11:2, 6, 39). That is why it says, "God is not ashamed to be called their God" (Hebrews 11:16). He was proud of them. To use the language of Proverbs 3:12, he delighted in them. When you are suffering, here is what you must remember: Your sufferings are not evidence against you, nor are they evidence against God. It is the opposite. Your sufferings are proof that God your Father cherishes you. As Hebrews 12:7 says, quoting these verses, "God is treating you as sons." Or as William Cowper wrote, "Behind a frowning providence He hides a smiling face."

Here is another way we can think of it. C. S. Lewis wisely proposed this in his book *The Problem of Pain*:

> Over a sketch made idly to amuse a child, an artist may not take much trouble; he may be content to let it go even though it is not exactly as he meant it to be. But over the great picture of his life . . . he will take endless trouble—and would, doubtless, thereby *give* endless trouble to the picture if it were sentient. One can imagine a sentient picture, after being rubbed and scraped and re-commenced for the tenth time, wishing that it were only a thumbnail sketch whose making was over in a minute. In the same way, it is natural for us to wish that God had designed for us a less glorious and less arduous destiny; but then we are wishing not for more love but for less.[7]

If you are in Christ and you are suffering, God does not hate you. If he did, he would not bother with you. The truth you need to know is this: You are a person of destiny, your greatness has already been won for you by Christ at his cross, and now God is getting you ready with some finishing touches, each one a masterstroke. If you could remove suffering not only from your own life but also from the whole world, you would not improve it. You would rob yourself of significance. You would create a world without the love of God. It would be a world where Jesus himself could not suffer and die for your or anyone's sins.

Maybe your own dad did not love you enough to discipline you, and now you feel that some blanks were never filled in here and there in your character. You do not like the way you are. But changing the way you are is not easy. Don't worry about it. You have a perfect Father in God, and he will help you along, step by step.

Second, *our wise pathway through suffering is to accept it and wait while God fulfills his purpose.* If you are suffering right now, you are probably being tempted in two opposite ways. Both are here in verse 11—either to despise the Lord's discipline, which is the active response of anger, or to be weary of his reproof, which is the passive response of despair. What is your only path forward? The Bible says, "[Be] trained by it" (Hebrews 12:11). We get our modern word *gymnasium* from that Greek word. By our sufferings, God has us working out. Is that so bad? Jesus himself suffered: "Although he was a son, he learned obedience through what he suffered" (Hebrews 5:8). The Bible says that Jesus sympathizes with our weaknesses, because he was tempted the same ways we are, but he did not sin. He neither lashed back at the Father, nor did he go limp (Hebrews 4:15). So we have a Friend in Jesus who is qualified to stand before God on our behalf but who is also sympathetic with us because he knows how it feels. So the Bible tells us what to do: "Let us then with confidence draw near to the throne of grace, that we may receive mercy and find grace to help in time of need" (Hebrews 4:16).

Here is what to ask for as you kneel there at the throne of grace. In Philippians 3:10 Paul said in essence, "I want to know Christ, and the power of his resurrection, and I want to share in the fellowship of his sufferings." Paul looked at the cross, he saw Jesus shedding his lifeblood for sinners, and Paul's heart said, "There is the wealth I want. There is the suffering I trust." Jesus is your treasure. Jesus is your approval. Will you believe that—yes, at that extreme of life where you find yourself right now?

8

Why Wisdom Matters, What Wisdom Creates

PROVERBS 3:13–35

Blessed is the one who finds wisdom,
and the one who gets understanding.

3:13

PROVERBS 3 EXPLAINS WHY wisdom matters and what wisdom creates. Wisdom matters, according to verses 13–26, because wisdom is the open secret of the universe. It is not a private option, take it or leave it. Wisdom is how life *works*. We can disregard that for a while and get away with it, because God built everything so well. But we want the last chapter of our stories to be the best, don't we? So wisdom matters. Wisdom also creates something, according to verses 27–35. Wisdom creates a culture of life amid this culture of death called our world. Wisdom is a community experience. It is a shared experience of life in its fullness. Let's go there together.

What every city needs is more churches where sinners are safe and people can live again, because the wisdom of Jesus rules in those churches. I grew up in that kind of church. If you too have experienced that kind of happy church, you know how wonderful it is. The only Biblical strategy for world redemption—the church—is undervalued even by some of God's own people. But God wants to take us into that promised land, and Proverbs 3 shows us the way. It requires of us more than good intentions, even more than Biblical doctrine. It requires the wisdom of God, embodied in more and more churches, so that people can see how wonderful life in Christ really is. Then they can join us and stop dying and start living, even forever. So much is at stake in the quality of our churches.

So the passage divides into these two main sections—verses 13–26, wisdom as the open secret of the universe, and verses 27–35, wisdom as a culture of life amid a culture of death. Let's think it through.

Wisdom: The Open Secret of the Universe
> Blessed is the one who finds wisdom,
>> and the one who gets understanding. (Proverbs 3:13)

The sage is telling us three things in verses 13–26. First, wisdom enriches everyone who finds it (vv. 13–18). We see the word "blessed" at the beginning of verse 13 and at the end of verse 18, marking these verses off as a paragraph. The key in this paragraph is easy to overlook. It is the two little words "the one" in verse 13: "Blessed is *the one* who finds wisdom." It is the Hebrew *'adam*, that is, generic "man," a human being, because wisdom is available to everyone.

There is such a thing as common grace, and there is such a thing as special grace. Common grace is the goodness of God that he showers universally on the human race. Jesus said, "[God] makes his sun rise on the evil and on the good, and sends rain on the just and on the unjust" (Matthew 5:45). God generously throws out onto this world many gifts on many people. All that is required for anyone to benefit from the wisdom of common grace is to get up and find it: "Blessed is the one, the anyone, who gets up and goes searching for wisdom until he finds it." But common grace, though common, is still God's grace. Wherever you see skill and expertise, you see a gift of God. John Calvin understood this:

> Whenever we come upon [giftedness] in secular writers, let that admirable light of truth shining in them teach us that the mind of man, though fallen and perverted from its wholeness, is nevertheless clothed and ornamented with God's excellent gifts. . . . Shall we count anything praiseworthy or noble without recognizing at the same time that it comes from God?[1]

When people excel in science, art, business, athletics, and so forth, it is because God made his wisdom available, and they got up and found it. For example, "Crazy" by Willie Nelson, sung by Patsy Cline. You do not have to like country music to know that song is two minutes and forty-one seconds of pure magic. Guess what? *God gave it*, in his common grace. Let's be thankful.

Where we go wrong with God's gifts is that we think they are about money: ". . . for the gain from [wisdom] is better than gain from silver and her profit better than gold" (v. 14). The sage is counseling us, "Don't aim at money. If you need money, aim at wisdom and you'll make the money that's right for you." That is why wisdom is "more precious than jewels" (v. 15). Wisdom is skill at living life well. Money is not. Money can put food on the table, but wisdom puts laughter around that table. Money can buy a house, but wisdom makes it a home. Money can buy a woman jewelry, but wisdom wins her heart.[2] All the ways of wisdom are "pleasantness" (v. 17). You cannot say that about money. We can wreck our lives by settling for the wisdom that does make us money when God is offering us the wisdom that takes us to "a tree of life" (v. 18). And that is no common grace. That tree of life feeds our hearts with the special grace of Jesus Christ. He died on the cross for geniuses who excel in earthly skills but are clueless about real life. Do not stop short. Do not settle for money. If you like money and silver and gold and jewels (vv. 14, 15), remember that they are mere metaphors for the life-giving special grace of Christ himself.

Second, wisdom matters to God, who uses it as his tool in both creation and providence (vv. 19, 20):

> The LORD by wisdom founded the earth;
>   by understanding he established the heavens;
> by his knowledge the deeps broke open,
>   and the clouds drop down the dew.

We have been told that the universe just happened. We have been told that we emerged out of the primordial goo by sheer luck. But the truth is, God created all things, and the tool he used was his own wisdom, and it was all he needed: "The LORD *by wisdom* founded the earth." At this very moment, he sustains—note the present tense "drop down" in verse 20—he sustains all things, even the dewdrops, by his wisdom. Dr. John Piper wrote about this rain in a Thanksgiving meditation a few years ago:

> Picture yourself as a farmer in the Near East, far from any lake or stream. A few wells keep the family and animals supplied with water. But if the crops are to grow and the family is to be fed from month to month, water has to come on the fields from another source. From where?
>   Well, the sky. The sky? Water will come out of the clear blue sky? Well, not exactly. Water will have to be carried in the sky from the Mediterranean Sea, over several hundred miles and then be poured out from the sky onto the fields. Carried? How much does it weigh? Well, if one inch of rain falls on one square mile of farmland during the night, that would

be 27,878,400 cubic feet of water, which is 206,300,160 gallons, which is 1,650,501,280 pounds of water.

That's heavy. So how does it get up in the sky and stay up there if it's so heavy? Well, it gets up there by evaporation. Really? That's a nice word. What's it mean? It means that the water sort of stops being water for a while so it can go up and not down. I see. Then how does it get down? Well, condensation happens. What's that? The water starts becoming water again by gathering around little dust particles between .00001 and .0001 centimeters wide. That's small.

What about the salt? Salt? Yes, the Mediterranean Sea is salt water. That would kill the crops. What about the salt? Well, the salt has to be taken out. Oh. So the sky picks up a billion pounds of water from the sea and takes out the salt and then carries it for three hundred miles and then dumps it on the farm?

Well, it doesn't dump it. If it dumped a billion pounds of water on the farm, the wheat would be crushed. So the sky dribbles the billion pounds water down in little drops. . . .[3]

The point is, if God by his wisdom can work that wonder in nature, what will he accomplish by his wisdom in you? We are surrounded and sustained by God's wisdom, though we barely understand it. C. S. Lewis explained why:

At present we are on the outside of the world, the wrong side of the door. We discern the freshness and purity of morning, but they do not make us fresh and pure. We cannot mingle with the splendors we see. But . . . some day, God willing, we shall get *in*.[4]

Jesus died to get us *in*. But even now we can see the creation for what it is—God's ingenious wisdom. Jonathan Edwards taught us a godly attitude toward life:

True virtue most essentially consists in a benevolence to Being in general. Or perhaps to speak more accurately, it is that consent, propensity and union of heart to Being in general, that is immediately exercised in a general good will.[5]

A general good will and appreciation of all God has made—that mentality is virtuous. But a crabby negativism is how we feel when our outsiderness is all we pay attention to. Some of us have lived in a foreign country, and we know how lonely it is to walk the streets of a city unable to read the signs, unable to ask for directions, because we do not know the language. We are like that in God's amazing creation. But God is translating his wisdom for us, supremely in Christ. That wisdom is the true foundation and meaning of the universe. He is urging us to take it to heart and to make it our own as outsiders who put our hope in him.

That is the third thing the sage is urging upon us, in verses 21–26, where he changes his style to direct address:

> My son, do not lose sight of these—
>   keep sound wisdom and discretion,
> and they will be life for your soul
>   and adornment for your neck
> . . . for the LORD will be your confidence
>   and will keep your foot from being caught. (Proverbs 3:21, 22, 26)

This paragraph is about personal safety. As we grow in wisdom, God protects us from the land mines that sin has hidden here in his world. The Lord himself is with us. That's how verse 26 can be translated. When we read, "the LORD will be your confidence," it means he will be our companion. The alternative translation of the Hebrew is, "The LORD will be at your side."[6] When the Apostle Paul was suffering, the Lord was at his side: "At my first defense no one came to stand by me, but all deserted me. May it not be charged against them! But the Lord stood by me and strengthened me" (2 Timothy 4:16, 17). The longer you and I live, the more stories we have to tell of the Lord standing at our side strengthening us. We are not trusting wisdom as an impersonal cosmic force; we are trusting the living Christ to stay close moment by moment, because he has promised, "I will be at your side."

That is the first section of the passage—why wisdom matters. Now in verses 27–35 the sage explains what wisdom creates here in God's magnificent world, which has been hijacked by stupidity and death. But the risen Jesus is pouring out his Spirit to create a new culture of life, called the church.

Wisdom: A Culture of Life amid a Culture of Death

The sage made three points in the first section, and now he makes three points in the second section about a new culture of life: help your needy neighbor, protect your innocent neighbor, avoid your violent neighbor. Let's break it down.

> Do not withhold good from those to whom it is due,
>   when it is in your power to do it.
> Do not say to your neighbor, "Go and come again,
>   tomorrow I will give it"—when you have it with you. (Proverbs 3:27, 28)

First, in a culture of life people help each other as much as they can. We cannot do the impossible. We cannot give what we do not have. But when it is in our power to do it, when we have it with us, wisdom says, "Give it away." The grace of Jesus taught the Apostle Paul to say, "I am a debtor" (Romans 1:14, NKJV). He did not see himself as a demander but a debtor. Nobody owed him a hearing. He won a hearing by loving people the way God loved him—graciously.

Let me show you how radical this is. Verse 27 says, "Do not withhold good from those to whom it is due." But also note the alternative translation in the ESV margin: "Do not withhold good from its *owners*." If you have good you can do for somebody, then legally you own it, but morally they own it. The state has no right to force you to be generous. And no one can walk into your house and start helping themselves to your things and say, "The Bible says I own it." What the Bible says to them is, "You shall not steal" (Exodus 20:15). But what the Bible says to you is, "You shall not withhold." We sin against each other not only by the bad things we do but also by the beautiful things we withhold. Withheld love is a life-depleting sin. It is a sin to tell ourselves, "I'm not doing anybody any *harm*." The question is, what *good* are you withholding? Jesus withheld no good thing from you. Okay, now we know how to build a culture of life, by his power. A culture of life is where people love each other openly and eagerly with the love of Jesus. All around us are opportunities to breathe life into more people. We cannot do everything. But we can do something, for his sake. If we have the ability, they have the ownership. And we owe it today, not tomorrow.

Second, in a culture of life people protect each other. The sage makes that positive point with his negative prohibitions:

Do not plan evil against your neighbor,
    who dwells trustingly beside you.
Do not contend with a man for no reason,
    when he has done you no harm. (Proverbs 3:29, 30)

Trust is the glue that holds community together. What do a husband and wife, for example, most need from each other? Trust. The Lord calls us to trust him unreservedly (v. 5), because trust is the platform on which a real relationship can happen. We all know what it is like to trust someone, and then he or she turns against us. That is painful, because trust is so profound. What then does wisdom say to us here? Negatively, do not be a faultfinding, critical person, ready to pounce on some well-meaning individual with a "Gotcha!" That is a culture of death. But Heaven has come down to us through Christ. He defended us when we deserved the opposite. So, let's stick up for our innocent neighbors. That is wisdom, creating a culture of safety in a world of attack.

Third, in a culture of life the wise keep their distance from the violent:

> Do not envy a man of violence
>> and do not choose any of his ways,
> for the devious person is an abomination to the LORD,
>> but the upright are in his confidence. (Proverbs 3:31, 32)

The way things are now, violent people succeed, and we are tempted to envy them. It starts early, with the bully on the playground who is also in the popular crowd. People fear and envy the violent. So the violent run the world. Remember the scene in *The Godfather Part 2* when young Vito Corleone is driving down the street in New York and the cheap hood Don Fanucci jumps into his car, gestures around, and snarls, "This is *my* neighborhood"? That is where the violence comes from: "This is my neighborhood, this is my office, this is my church, this is my world—*not yours*." God says in verse 32, "That's an *abomination*." In other words, it turns God's stomach. But God loves to defend those whom no one else defends. He is involved in this world. He is not standing aloof. He is no bystander or spectator. Whatever abuse you suffer, no one can take this from you: "The upright are in his confidence" (v. 32). Being close to Christ is better than being on top of the world. He has all authority in Heaven and on earth. If they drive you out, the Lord will take you in. "Toward the scorners he is scornful, but to the humble he gives favor" (v. 34). He is wise enough to know how to subvert subversive people and also build you up. Humble yourself and trust him with all your heart.

The Septuagint translates verse 34 in a way you might be familiar with: "God opposes the proud, but gives grace to the humble" (quoted in James 4:6; 1 Peter 5:5). We can and will do that, depending on how we understand verse 35, the final verse in the passage: "The wise will inherit honor, but fools get disgrace." Your everything depends on how you read that verse. Who *are* "the wise"? Who *are* the "fools"? Who really are the winners and losers in this world? Whose stock is rising, whose stock is falling? How you answer that question reveals everything about you, because how you answer that question reveals how you see the cross of Jesus. From one point of view, the cross is for losers and failures and weaklings and outsiders. From the opposite point of view, the cross represents everything to be trusted, admired, embraced.

What about you? How do *you* feel about that man hanging on the cross, that man betrayed, excluded, humiliated by this brilliant world? How you feel about that crucified man reveals who you are at your deepest core, whether wise or foolish, because in fact his stock is rising now and forever in resurrection power. Here is the future: the wise in Christ will inherit the honor of Christ. Why not become a part of that?

9

The Only Path into Life

PROVERBS 4:1–27

Let your heart hold fast my words;
keep my commandments, and live.

4:4

Keep hold of instruction; do not let go;
guard her, for she is your life.

4:13

Keep your heart with all vigilance,
for from it flow the springs of life.

4:23

PROVERBS 4 IS NOT PRIMARILY ABOUT DON'TS, though they have their place. We cannot say yes to everything. But this very positive chapter is about how we can *live*. Jesus said, "I came that they may have life and have it abundantly" (John 10:10). Every one of us wants that. We do not deserve it. But we can have it, to the max, because Christ gives it, on terms of grace. Gardiner Spring, in a sermon on James 1:17 ("Every good gift and every perfect gift is from above, coming down from the Father of lights"), said this:

> Other sources of enjoyment there are, but He is the great Source; other givers there are, but He is the great Giver. The sun gives its light, the clouds their rain, the earth its fruits, the sea its treasures; angels give; men are

givers; yet of all givers in the universe, God is the greatest—the Father of lights and of mercies, Himself the source, the contriver, the dispenser of every "good gift and every perfect gift." . . . God is the greatest of givers.[1]

The gospel is not about what we give to God but what he gives to us—true life in all its richness and fullness. And no matter who you are, you can have it all freely, beginning today, through Christ. His gospel is so inviting.

Thomas Chalmers was a minister in the Church of Scotland about two hundred years ago. In his famous sermon entitled "The Expulsive Power of a New Affection,"[2] he offered a keen insight. Even when we see the stupidity of our sins and how empty they are and how they only make us sad, that realization still does not change us. We start changing only when we see Christ, when we see that Christ will make us alive in ways our most darling sins cannot, when we see that in Christ we are not losing anything but our damnation and gaining everything we desire in our own deepest intentions. The gospel shows us Jesus pouring out his lifeblood, so that we can live. The gospel says, "Look at him. Come to him. Follow him. You will stop dying, you will start living, and it will never end." As the church we want to stop dying so much and start living more and more. We want that for everyone around us too.

Proverbs 4 shows us the only path into life: Christ. The chapter breaks down like this: how to get going (vv. 1–9), how to keep going (vv. 10–19), and how not to get lost along the way (vv. 20–27).

How to Get Going

Hear, O sons, a father's instruction,
  and be attentive, that you may gain insight,
for I give you good precepts;
  do not forsake my teaching.
When I was a son with my father,
  tender, the only one in the sight of my mother,
he taught me and said to me,
"Let your heart hold fast my words;
  keep my commandments, and live." (Proverbs 4:1–4)

We are overhearing a father of teenage sons coaching them in wisdom. How does he do it? He tells them what he learned when he himself was a boy. He is saying, "I remember when I was a kid, how my dad got me going into a great life." We have seen this father/son conversation before.[3] But now we meet the grandfather. Now we see three generations in the family. Evidently the grandfather has died, because the father does not say, "Remember what grandpa used to say?" Instead the father informs his sons about how his dad made such a positive impact during his youth. So do you see? We are being invited into a *tradition* of wisdom.

What is tradition? Tradition is previous generations handing down to us something of their own. Our forefathers are not disqualified from speaking into our lives just by the accident of their death.[4] In fact, they have an advantage over us. They fought the good fight, they finished the race, they kept the faith (2 Timothy 4:7). On my ordination certificate are twenty-five signatures. In 1975 all those men were faithful to Christ. But today one of them is a radical gay activist, and another is under suspicion by the LAPD for murdering his wife, and he looks guilty as sin. You and I today are less than fully proven. So those who have already gone the distance have something to say that we do not. Proverbs 4 is alerting us to the value of past voices.

Let's think, just briefly and selectively, about what we stand to gain from our tradition as Christians. It has been 2,000 years since Jesus—maybe sixty generations, if we figure about thirty-three years per generation. About twelve generations into this historical flow along came a man named Augustine. He taught us that God made us for himself, and our hearts are restless until we find our rest in him. And Augustine did find that rest. About thirty-two generations into this flow, along came a man named Anselm. He taught us that until we come to Christ, we cannot know what a heavy weight sin is. And for Anselm, that weight was lifted away. About forty-five generations into it, along came a man named Martin Luther. He taught us that God treats bad people like good people through the finished work of Christ on the cross, received with mere faith. And Luther entered into that grace. About fifty-three generations into it, along came a man named Jonathan Edwards. He taught us that real Christianity is a miracle, as God powerfully awakens dead hearts with new affections for Christ. And God gave that miracle to Edwards. About fifty-nine generations into it, along came a man named Ray Ortlund Sr. He taught me what a revival-ready church looks like. And God honored his readiness with the reality. The Bible says, "Remember your leaders, those who spoke to you the word of God. Consider the outcome of their way of life, and imitate their faith" (Hebrews 13:7). We do not have to imitate their style, but we would be fools not to imitate their faith. It took them all the way into *life*. This is why C. S. Lewis said that, after reading a modern book, we should not read another one until we have read at least one old book.[5] The Old Dead Guys speak from proven experience.

What are all these generations telling us? "Jesus didn't fail us, and he won't fail you. Go for it!" So this father here in Proverbs 4 is looking deeply into the eyes of his dear son and urging him to set his heart firmly on the only prize in all this world that cannot fail:

Get wisdom; get insight . . .
The beginning of wisdom is this: get wisdom,
    and whatever you get, get insight. (Proverbs 4:5a, 7)

Do you feel that urgency about getting wisdom for yourself? Are you convinced yet? My first-year Greek textbook quoted Dr. Samuel Johnson as saying, "Greek, Sir, is like lace; every man gets as much of it as he can."[6] Back then a proper gentleman adorned his persona with Greek and with lace. How quaint. Maybe you feel that way about wisdom, but you have more urgent goals elsewhere. But God your Father is looking into your eyes with great love as his own child and saying this to you right now: "Whatever you get, get insight."

The NIV clarifies the force of that: "*Though it cost all you have*, get understanding." If you want God's wisdom, it will cost you. It will cost you all your preconceived ideas about how life is supposed to work. Why pay that price? Because God's wisdom will make you alive (v. 4), his wisdom will "keep" you and "guard" you (v. 6), his wisdom will "exalt" you and "honor" you and crown you with beauty (vv. 8, 9). That is how life really works, and that is a life worth living! Who else can promise you that? Every day we are being told that, if we want to *live*, we need to be young, thin, tanned, sexually active, rich, and smart-mouthed. There is our cultural ideal, the wisdom of our age. Just one question. Is it working? If you actually got hold of all that, would you walk away from it a complete human being? All those young, thin, tanned, sexually active, rich, smart-mouthed people—name one person who has thrown himself into that life and come away from it with what you want for yourself. Name *one*. And how do you explain 2,000 years of all types of people from different cultures who set their hearts on Christ, turned to his wisdom in the Bible, and found fullness of life?

You face a choice today—the proven way of Christ versus the defunct way of man. *Whichever you choose, it will cost you all you have.* But which path will give you everything you want? Jesus is so gracious. To follow him, you do not need to measure up to a cultural ideal of youth and cool. But you do need to become decisive. Though it cost you all you have, and it will, get Christ. Don't you feel that something in your life needs to change? Don't you need to turn a corner? Don't you want newness of life from Christ? Well, come and get it. Decisiveness is all you need to get going.

How to Keep Going

> But the path of the righteous is like the light of dawn,
>> which shines brighter and brighter until full day. (Proverbs 4:18)

The key metaphor in this second paragraph is "the way." Verse 11: "the way of wisdom . . . the paths of uprightness." Verse 14: "the path of the wicked . . . the way of the evil." Verse 18: "the path of the righteous." Verse 19: "the way of the wicked." We face only two alternatives—the wise way or the evil way. In our hobbit-like timidity we might prefer a compromise. We might prefer three ways to choose from—a rotten life of folly over at one extreme, a super-duper life of wisdom over at the other extreme, but in the middle a half-decent life of mediocrity that we don't mind settling for. But God is saying there are only two ways: a gloomy disaster of a life without his wisdom and a bright success of a life with his wisdom. Therefore, God's wisdom is not an optional extra: ". . . she is your life" (v. 13).

What does the path metaphor tell us? It tells us that life is a journey, there is no quick fix, and we take it one step at a time with constant, moment-by-moment recommitments to the way of Christ. As we go forward on this path, the sage has a warning for us, and he has hope for us.

Now he gives us his warning. And it is not a threat. He is not saying, "Here are my arbitrary rules to control you. Keep them *or else.*" He is simply explaining that one of these two paths leads into a minefield:

> Do not enter the path of the wicked,
>> and do not walk in the way of the evil.
> Avoid it; do not go on it;
>> turn away from it and pass on.
> For they cannot sleep unless they have done wrong;
>> they are robbed of sleep unless they have made someone stumble.
> For they eat the bread of wickedness
>> and drink the wine of violence. (Proverbs 4:14–17)

Evil becomes compulsive, and none of us is above it, because this is the nature of our depraved hearts. Jesus said, "Everyone who commits sin is a slave to sin" (John 8:34). Sin is a slavery deep inside, an emotional engine we cannot shut down just by choosing to do so. How do we see this dynamic at work today? Think of politics. Human politics is not just about winning; it is about destroying the other person, and there is no stopping it. Think of the gambling industry, with its antisocial impact, but there is no stopping it. We scarcely understand the dark powers we unleash inside ourselves when we turn one step away from the path of Christ's wisdom. Remember how Satan thought, that dark new thought that formed in his mind, in Milton's *Paradise Lost* when Satan gave up on God:

> So farewell hope, and with hope farewell fear,
> Farewell remorse; all good to me is lost;
> Evil, be thou my good. . . .[7]

The wise father, the sage in Proverbs 4, is warning us that we will be tempted, and behind every temptation is an overwhelming power of darkness and despair. So let's realize how much is at stake in what we choose. And the best defense is a good offense—our hope in Christ.

That is the second thing the sage wants us to see here—our bright hope in the promise of the gospel:

> But the path of the righteous is like the light of dawn,
>   which shines brighter and brighter until full day. (Proverbs 4:18)

What keeps us moving forward in the way of God's wisdom is hope, confidence, expectancy. You might not be much of a Christian right now. Who of us is? But if you have chosen Christ, he is dawning in your life. There might be only a glimmer of light on your horizon right now. But the sun is rising, the darkness cannot stop it, and Christ will bring his good work in you to noonday brilliance: "He who began a good work in you will bring it to completion at the day of Jesus Christ" (Philippians 1:6). That bright gospel confidence is how you keep going, step by step, moment by moment, on the right path.

How Not to Get Lost along the Way

> Keep your heart with all vigilance,
>   for from it flow the springs of life. (Proverbs 4:23)

In this final paragraph the sage calls us to pay attention to every step we take. He is calling us to concentrated focus. A lack of self-awareness will get us lost. But we keep making progress toward the high noon of our most fervent hopes by applying the gospel to our hearts constantly.

The counsel of verse 23 is wise—and opposite to the wisdom of our age. We are told today that if we are going to be happy, what we need to do is assemble around us our selfish little designer life just the way we want it, with our dream house and our trophy wife and our ideal job and all the rest. But the truth is, if we got it all, it would only make us more depressed and angry, because all those outward advantages would only mock our sadness within. *Life does not flow from the outside in; it flows from the inside out.* We need our hearts continuously filled with the ever-fresh life of Christ, by faith in the gospel. I think Jesus had this verse in mind when he said, "If anyone thirsts, let him come to me and drink. Whoever believes in me, as the Scripture has said, 'Out of his heart will flow rivers of living water'" (John 7:37, 38). We will not lose our way on the journey of life if we will keep coming to Jesus and drinking in his acceptance, his forgiveness, his promises, his love. Everything else flows out from deep in there.

In her book *Women, Food and God*, Geneen Roth, who is not writing as a Christian, gets close to the truth:

> Women turn to food when they are not hungry because they *are* hungry for something they can't name: a connection to what is beyond the concerns of daily life. Something deathless, something sacred. But replacing the hunger for divine connection with Double Stuf Oreos is like giving a glass of sand to a person dying of thirst. It creates more thirst, more panic.[8]

Your heart has a hunger, a thirst, that only Christ can satisfy. And he can, overflowingly, forever, freely, for you. Come. Come as you are. Come moment by moment. Drink him in.

What about us men? We need to guard our hearts too. What are we looking at on our computers and taking into our hearts? Remember the old Greek myth of Medusa? Anyone who just looked at her turned to stone. Alexander Pope told us how our hearts can become hardened:

> Vice is a monster of so frightful mien
> As, to be hated, needs but to be seen;
> Yet seen too oft, familiar with her face,
> We first endure, then pity, then embrace.[9]

Don't cram your heart full of death. Fill your heart with the love of Jesus for sinful men by believing the gospel moment by moment. As we draw the love we crave from Jesus, it flows out in healing throughout our beings. Look how the sage makes it practical by referring to the various parts of our bodies:

> Put away from you a crooked *mouth*,
>   and put devious *lips* far from you.[10]
> Let your *eyes* look directly forward,
>   and your gaze be straight before you.
> Ponder the path of your *feet*;
>   then all your ways will be sure.
> Do not swerve to the right or to the left;
>   turn your *foot* away from evil. (Proverbs 4:24–27)

The Lord Jesus Christ who died for you also claims you, all that you are from head to toe. The gospel calls you to deploy your very body for him: "I appeal to you therefore, brothers, by the mercies of God, to present your bodies as a living sacrifice, holy and acceptable to God, which is your spiritual worship" (Romans 12:1). If we are distracted from real-time connection with the mercies of God, so that our hearts grow cold and our mouths become reckless and our eyes wayward and our feet wandering, we are only one misstep away from life-shattering catastrophe. We do not have to give ourselves to raw evil to end up there; we only have to un-guard our hearts, we only have to stop being vigilant. Every one of us is always five minutes away from total disaster. But if we are receiving by faith the outpouring of Christ's love in constant supply from his Throne of Grace, we cannot lose our way.

Let's make this concrete. If you are right-handed, hold your right hand in front of you so that you can look at it. If you are left-handed, hold out your left hand. You do a lot with that hand, both good and evil. But now dedicate that hand to Christ. He can make you wise all your life long with that hand. Here is what you need to remember: Jesus died for your hand. Yes, your hand. And he did not die only for the sins you have committed with that hand. He shed his blood out of love for your hand, to redeem your hand, to make your hand wise in the present and immortal in the future, to the praise of the glory of his grace. Someday your hand will be powerful for God such as you cannot imagine right now. Your hand will no longer feel pain. Your hand will no longer be able to sin. Your hand will touch the hand of Christ. In fact, *everything* you are will be redeemed. Still more, *the whole creation* "will be set free from its bondage to corruption and obtain the freedom of the glory of the children of God" (Romans 8:21). If you are in Christ, that massive liberation will include you, all of you, everything about you. How can you give yourself over to stupidity now? That is not your path. That is not your destiny. Christ has set you apart to himself. Christ will have the final say in your life, and his purpose of grace is dawning in you right now.

Will you consecrate your hand, and everything you are, to Christ and his wisdom? If you will keep your heart with all vigilance for his sake, Christ will fill you with his springs of life. With a heart filled by Christ, you will not lose your way.

10

Bitter Honey and Sweet Water[1]

PROVERBS 5:1–23

Let your fountain be blessed,
and rejoice in the wife of your youth,
a lovely deer, a graceful doe.
Let her breasts fill you at all times with delight;
be intoxicated always in her love.

5:18, 19

ONE OF THE BENEFITS OF PREACHING through a section of the Bible is that the Bible itself raises topics we might otherwise avoid, like sex. The Bible is not shy about sex, and its message is clear: sexual folly destroys, sexual wisdom satisfies, and Christ is better than the best sex.

Proverbs 5 divides into three parts. In the introduction (vv. 1–6), God our Father lovingly says, "It's time we had a talk." In the body of the chapter (vv. 7–19), God says, "Here is what I want you to know." He is very down-to-earth. In the conclusion (vv. 20–23), God says, "Now you have a decision to make." God speaks into every area of our lives, including our sexuality. The introduction opens up that conversation with us. The body of the chapter contrasts the two ways we can deploy our sexuality—either in folly and destruction or in wisdom and satisfaction. The conclusion calls us to surrender ourselves entirely to God and to his wisdom.

Here is the key concept we must understand, and it applies to all of life: The gospel calls us into both form and freedom, both structure and liberation. Conservative people love form and restraint and control, especially in sex.

Progressive people love freedom and openness and choices, especially in sex. Both see part of the truth, but the gospel tells us the whole truth. And the truth is, God gave us our sexuality both to focus our romantic joy and to unleash our romantic joy. When this very human joy is both focused and unleashed—having both form and freedom—it becomes wonderfully intensified. We *thrive* within both form and freedom. Sex is like fire. In the fireplace it keeps us warm. Outside the fireplace it burns the house down. Proverbs 5 is saying, "Keep the fire in the marital fireplace, and stoke that fire as hot as you can."

I will stick carefully to what the Bible itself is saying. I will neither sensationalize it nor mute it. Let's all receive the word of God and be saved by its wonderful impact.

It's Time We Had a Talk

My son, be attentive to my wisdom;
    incline your ear to my understanding,
that you may keep discretion,
    and your lips may guard knowledge.
For the lips of a forbidden woman drip honey,
    and her speech is smoother than oil,
but in the end she is bitter as wormwood,
    sharp as a two-edged sword.
Her feet go down to death;
    her steps follow the path to Sheol;
she does not ponder the path of life;
    her ways wander, and she does not know it. (Proverbs 5:1–6)

This wise father is saying to his son, "You're going to be tempted. You're walking into a world of sexual foolishness. It will be offered to you as honey, and you will be attracted. But this honey will poison you." Note the word "honey" in verse 3 and the word "bitter" in verse 4. Honey is sweet. So whatever leaves a bitter aftertaste in your mouth cannot be honey. Don't be fooled. Don't judge by the appearances of the moment. The lasting impact tomorrow and thereafter reveals the truth about the present moment. Her words may ooze seductive charm—face-to-face, on the Internet, in a text message; but her sweet talk and her flattery, telling you how awesome you are and how she's been looking for a man just like you, that "honey" will turn "bitter." And more than your sexuality is at stake; verse 5 says "her feet go down to *death*," spiritually and even literally. We in Nashville remember our Titans' quarterback Steve McNair being shot to death by the girl with whom he was having an affair. Sexual integrity is life versus death. Everything you care about is on the line!

If you are a woman, I would not blame you if you thought, "These verses are unfair. Men can be just as bad as women." True. And the book of Proverbs warns us against evil men too (for example, 1:10–19). But no one passage can say everything. Plus, when the sexually foolish man comes to his senses in verse 13, whom does he blame? "*I* did not listen to the voice of my teachers." He blames himself. So the father-figure speaking here is not being one-sided in his outlook.

Why is God our Father having this talk with us today? Because we too are vulnerable. If you think you are above sexual stupidity, you are asking for it. If you know you're not above it, you might be helped and strengthened by reading Mark Driscoll's book *Porn-Again Christian*. It is a free download from relit.org.[2] It will squeeze a drop of bitter wormwood onto your tongue, so to speak, so that you ponder the path of your feet (v. 6) in our world of sexual chaos.

God wants to give us the wonderful gift of sexual wisdom. His introduction, in verses 1–6, is a blunt warning. In the body of the chapter he has a two-part message: "Keep your hands *off* every other woman" (vv. 7–14), "Keep your hands *on* your wife" (vv. 15–19).

Here's What I Want You to Know

> And now, O sons, listen to me,
>   and do not depart from the words of my mouth.
> Keep your way far from her,
>   and do not go near the door of her house,
> lest you give your honor to others
>   and your years to the merciless,
> lest strangers take their fill of your strength,
>   and your labors go to the house of a foreigner,
> and at the end of your life you groan,
>   when your flesh and body are consumed. (Proverbs 5:7–11)

Verse 8 is the key: "Keep your way *far* from her." Don't tell yourself you can get involved just a little and then get clear, no big deal, and nobody will ever know. Martyn Lloyd-Jones told us how life really works:

> Be careful how you treat God, my friends. You may say to yourself, "I can sin against God and then, of course, I can repent and go back and find God whenever I want him." You try it. And you will sometimes find that not only can you not find God but that you do not even want to. You will be aware of a terrible hardness in your heart. And you can do nothing about it. And then you suddenly realize that it is God punishing you in order to reveal your sinfulness and your vileness to you. And there is only one thing to do. You turn back to him and you say, "O God, do not go on dealing with me

judicially, though I deserve it. Soften my heart. Melt me. I cannot do it myself." You cast yourself utterly upon his mercy and upon his compassion.[3]

Do you think you can play with sin and keep it under your control? Do you think you can compartmentalize God? Sexual folly complicates *everything*, as these verses say. When we disobey God, our hearts harden. The other people we violate become hardened and embittered toward us, because sooner or later they find out too. That is the point of verses 9–11—the wider impact of sexual folly. It depletes a man financially in cover-ups and alimony and lawsuits, socially in his reputation, emotionally in his conscience, and of course in his marriage. Jealousy, hurt, loneliness, regret—the cost is high. Satan shows the bait, but he hides the hook. Verse 9 says we men can end up giving our years to "the merciless." When Proverbs was written, the author probably had in mind the husband offended by an adulterous affair, with his relatives and friends taking his side against the offender. That can happen today too. But in addition the porn industry is merciless. It wants to enslave us. Verse 11 says, "And at the end of your life you groan." It doesn't take long for the pain and the groaning to begin. Lord Byron was the bad boy of the nineteenth century whom everyone secretly envied. He was in Greece on his thirty-sixth birthday, all alone. Here is what he wrote:

My days are in the yellow leaf,
The flowers and fruits of love are gone;
The worm, the canker, and the grief
Are mine alone![4]

In other words, "I'm thirty-six, and I'm already old. All I have left is VD and depression. Where are my drinking buddies now, when I need them?"

There is only one true Friend for sexual fools. His name is Jesus Christ, the Crucified One. He wants you to know that your sexuality is a magnificent gift from God, for his glory and your blessing. What you are, as a created being, is not fundamentally a problem; what you are, man or woman, is fundamentally a privilege. But if you used your iPhone, this highly sophisticated communications technology, to hammer nails, you would show complete incomprehension of an iPhone. Even so, your sexuality is a powerful, delicate gift from God. You cannot violate his gift without damaging repercussions. So the Lord wants us to know something else. There is a way back to healing, and that way is humility. Note how the tune changes in verses 12–14:

. . . "How I hated discipline,
and my heart despised reproof!

I did not listen to the voice of my teachers
   or incline my ear to my instructors.
I am at the brink of utter ruin.
   in the assembled congregation." (Proverbs 5:12–14)

The sexually foolish man finally faces himself. He owns up, like the prodigal son (Luke 15:11–24). That young man in Jesus' parable looked at himself and how low he had fallen and he said, "I am at the brink of utter ruin. But I have a father. I have a home. Why stay here?" He got up and went home. And while he was still a long way off, his father ran to him and kissed him. The father did not shame him but rejoiced over him. You may be a long way off too. Maybe you're stalling. But what are you waiting for? You have a Father. You have a home. The world may pick up its skirts and pass you by. The world may say you belong in the gutter. But God your Father, because of the cross, is ready to embrace you—yes, you in your rags, in your mess, as you are right now. Will you come home to him today? He will receive you and rejoice over you and renew you. He will give you your virginity back, plus more. The Bible says, "If anyone is in Christ, he is a new creation. The old has passed away; behold, the new has come" (2 Corinthians 5:17). The Bible says, "You were washed, you were sanctified, you were justified in the name of the Lord Jesus Christ and by the Spirit of our God" (1 Corinthians 6:11). Our Savior is making "all things *new*" (Revelation 21:5).

Now, as the body of the chapter unfolds, here is the message of God's wonderful gift of sexual wisdom:

Drink water from your own cistern,
   flowing water from your own well.
Should your springs be scattered abroad,
   streams of water in the streets?
Let them be for yourself alone,
   and not for strangers with you. (Proverbs 5:15–17)

The metaphor is water, to satisfy a raging thirst. The Bible is talking about a man's sexual desires, his passions and his powers. And God is saying, "Satisfy your thirst through lovemaking with your wife." Look what the Lord is *not* saying. He is *not* saying, "There's temptation out there? Then what you need is a will of iron. You need steely determination. So here is your future—endless frustration bottled up inside." Obviously we all need self-control if we are going to have emotional structures above a five-year-old level. Verse 23 warns against a "lack of discipline." But God's remedy for your thirst for sex is sex, overflowing sexual joy with your wife. That is what he means in verse 15 by "your own cistern" and "your own well." Your wife is your own personal and private, divinely approved wellspring of endless sexual satisfaction.

You have every right, therefore, to see by faith God your Father raising his hands in blessing over your marriage bed. I say that because verse 18 now adds a prayer. The wise father-figure prays over the married sexual experience of his son and daughter-in-law:

> May[5] your fountain be blessed,
>   and rejoice in the wife of your youth,
>   a lovely deer, a graceful doe.
> Let her breasts fill you at all times with delight;
>   be intoxicated always in her love.
> Why should you be intoxicated, my son, with a forbidden woman
>   and embrace the bosom of an adulteress? (Proverbs 5:18–20)

What does the prayed-for blessing of God look like? A spring of joyously bubbling sexual happiness between husband and wife. And that is sexual wisdom. Even as the years go by, she will always be "the wife of your youth." You will always cherish her and rejoice over her as that dear girl who gave herself completely to you alone. The "lovely deer, graceful doe" imagery of verse 19 is culturally remote from us. I *hunt* deer! But what the author has in mind is "their bright black eyes, their graceful limbs, and their irresistible silky hair," as Bruce Waltke explains in his commentary.[6] Husband, enjoy your wife visually. Honor and enjoy her beauty. Wife, present yourself to your husband as attractively as you can, lovely and graceful. How can you beautify yourself for your husband? Of all the women on the face of the earth today, you are the *only* morally legitimate satisfaction of his thirst for sexual enjoyment. Why not ask your husband, "Darling, how can I please you more?" Husband, when your wife sweetly asks you that question, she is making herself vulnerable. The first thing you should say is, "Well, for starters let me tell you the nineteen ways you absolutely thrill me! But since you ask, yes, here is one change that would be quite wonderful. . . ."

Verse 19 is frankly erotic. The verse is emphasizing two things: the quality of married lovemaking ("fill . . . with delight" and "be intoxicated") and the quantity of married lovemaking ("at all times" and "always"). The Bible is saying, "When you get married, drop your inhibitions, and *go for it* in both quality and quantity." That is a command of God. Back in the days of the Puritans—they were trying to be Biblical—when a New England wife complained, first to her pastor and then to the whole congregation, that her husband was neglecting their sex life, the church removed him as a member![7]

The Bible says, "The wife does not have authority over her own body, but the husband does. Likewise the husband does not have authority over his own body, but the wife does. Do not deprive one another" (1 Corinthians 7:4, 5). And Proverbs 5 is adding, "Make it fun and frequent!" The word translated "be intoxicated" is used elsewhere for a man staggering down the street in drunkenness (Isaiah 28:7). The point is to be *crazy* in love together. That is the good and wise will of God. And this comes from ancient times, when many marriages were arranged for economic and political purposes. But the Bible calls us to being head-over-heels in romantic love. The Bible values this so highly that verse 20 presses the point further by asking, Why throw that away? God is giving you your own personal Garden of Eden with your wife. Enjoy her—to the max.

But the ultimate reason for obeying God with sexual wisdom is not physical or social but spiritual. That is the final thing, and the most important thing, the wise father wants to say.

Now Decide!

For a man's ways are before the eyes of the LORD,
    and he ponders all his paths.
The iniquities of the wicked ensnare him,
    and he is held fast in the cords of his sin.
He dies for lack of discipline,
    and because of his great folly he is led astray. (Proverbs 5:21–23)

All of us are sexual sinners at some level, and we all know the slavery of it, the inescapable regret and shame of it. Sin touches everything we are. None of us is perfect. None of us is strong. We all need merciful liberation from our pasts. A friend who has professional expertise in this area tells me the estimates are that about 85 percent of men have premarital sex, after marrying about 25 percent of men and 15 percent of women commit adultery at some point, and about half of men and a third of women are looking at Internet porn once a month. A tsunami of sexual destruction is slamming us in our modern world today. We need a massive cleansing that only God can give. What can and must we do? *We must run to Christ, the mighty Friend of sexual fools.* Will you come to Christ right now, as you are, open to his grace and mercy for you?

Let's all hear the gospel again. Martin Luther explained it in terms of marriage, as the Bible so often does:

Faith . . . unites the soul with Christ, as a bride is united with her bridegroom. From such a marriage, as St. Paul says, it follows that Christ and the soul . . . hold all things in common, whether for better or worse. This means that what Christ possesses belongs to the believing soul, and what the soul possesses belongs to Christ. Thus Christ possesses all good things and holiness; these now belong to the soul. The soul possesses lots of vices and sin; these now belong to Christ. . . . Now is not this a happy business? Christ, the rich, noble and holy bridegroom, takes in marriage this poor, contemptible and sinful little prostitute, takes away all her evil and bestows all his goodness upon her! It is no longer possible for sin to overwhelm her, for she is now found in Christ.[8]

Come to Christ and be forgiven. Come to Christ and learn sexual wisdom as a gift of his grace.

11

Responsibility, Opportunity, Unity

PROVERBS 6:1–19

There are six things that the LORD hates,
seven that are an abomination to him . . .
one who sows discord among brothers.

6:16, 19

WE DO NOT COME TO CHURCH TO FINE-TUNE our own righteousness or to airbrush our appearances. We come because we want to grow and change. We want to know as much about God as he will tell us; we want to know as much about ourselves as he will tell us. We want his extreme grace for our extreme makeover, one step at a time. Proverbs 6:1–19 shows three steps God wants us to take.

God speaks here into three areas of our lives—how we handle money (vv. 1–5), how we discipline ourselves (vv. 6–11), and how we build community (vv. 12–19). He uses negative examples to teach us positive wisdom. His thought seems to progress from a bad example in verses 1–5, to a worse example in verses 6–11, to the worst example in verses 12–19. First, the wise father-figure speaks *to* his son who needs correction. We see "my son" in verses 1 and 3. Then the father speaks *to* the sluggard (v. 6), but he does not call him a son. Finally the father speaks *about* a disruptive person, without even addressing him. In fact, the father feels so strongly about community-destroyers that he doubles up on this third bad example. Verses 12–19 break down into two parts, verses 12–15 and verses 16–19, but the theme is the same: "continually sowing discord" (v. 14), "one who sows discord" (v. 19). God our Father is calling us to take new steps of faith and repentance into responsibility, opportunity, and unity, for the sake of Christ.

Responsibility

> My son, if you have put up security for your neighbor,
>   have given your pledge for a stranger,
> if you are snared in the words of your mouth,
>   caught in the words of your mouth,
> then do this, my son, and save yourself,
>   for you have come into the hand of your neighbor:
>   go, humble yourself,[1] and plead urgently with your neighbor.
> Give your eyes no sleep
>   and your eyelids no slumber;
> save yourself like a gazelle from the hand of the hunter,
>   like a bird from the hand of the fowler. (Proverbs 6:1–5)

What is "putting up security" or "giving your pledge" for someone else? It is cosigning a loan. It is putting yourself up as collateral. It is underwriting someone else's speculative risk. It is getting into a partnership when your partner's default can bring you down. God is saying in verses 1 and 2, "If you've done this, you're not *in danger of* becoming ensnared, you're *already* ensnared." Even the Federal Trade Commission, on its website, warns us about cosigning:

> You are being asked to guarantee this debt. Think carefully before you do. If the borrower does not pay the debt, you will have to. Be sure you can afford to pay if you have to, and that you want to accept this responsibility.
>
> You may have to pay up to the full amount of the debt if the borrower does not pay. You may also have to pay late fees or collection costs, which increase this amount.
>
> The creditor can collect this debt from you without first trying to collect from the borrower. The creditor can use the same collection methods against you that can be used against the borrower, such as suing you, garnishing your wages, etc. If this debt is ever in default, that fact may become a part of your credit record.[2]

If the person applying qualified for credit in the first place, he or she wouldn't be asking for someone else's backing, right?

The Bible is clear in two ways. One, God wants us to be generous. Two, God does not want us to gamble. The Old Testament commanded a culture of generosity. In Deuteronomy 15:1–12 God told his people to loan money to the poor freely, and every seven years all debts in the nation were canceled, erased forever. God had been generous to his people, so he wanted them to create a culture of generosity here within a world of tight-fisted, grudging exactitude. In the New Testament, when the Apostle Paul sent Onesimus back to Philemon, he said, "If he has wronged you at all, or owes you anything, charge that to my account" (Philemon 18). Paul covered Onesimus' past debts. But Paul did not promise to cover any future debts. That is the warning here in Proverbs 6 when it says not to "put up security for your neighbor."

God wants every one of us to take responsibility for himself. But if you put your financial future in the hands of someone the banks already think is a bad risk, you are acting irresponsibly yourself and encouraging irresponsibility in the other person. Look how serious this is. Look at the urgency of verses 3–5. God is saying, "Take decisive action. Get out of that obligation before it's too late!" The Hebrew verb translated "humble yourself" in verse 3 suggests getting down on the ground and letting the other guy trample all over you and call you every bad name, but you go ahead and let him do it and admit how stupid you have been, but get yourself free. The verb translated "plead urgently" means to pester, to badger.[3] It means leaving a string of messages on the answering machine. But just *hoping* things will work out is foolish.

A friend of mine made this mistake. He was at home one day when a man came by to ask him to cosign a loan for $250,000. The bank wanted more security. My friend thought, "He's a good guy, I care about him, I don't want to disappoint him," and he signed it. He knew Proverbs 6, but at that moment he forgot it. Then the man went belly-up, and the bank came after my friend. He lost about $100,000 in cash. And the bank did not let up on him until he begged them not to throw his wife out of their house. He had jeopardized his wife's future. He repented before God, and over the next ten years or so God graciously restored the lost money. It was pure grace.

If you are in a credit arrangement holding you hostage, you must get free. Take back your own responsibility for your life. Or if you have asked someone else to do this for you, you need to set him free.

Here is the good news for every one of us. In the book of Job, that suffering saint says to God, "Be my surety . . . for who else will pledge himself for me?" (Job 17:3, REB). In other words, "God, I'm a bad risk. I need you to do for me what I wouldn't do for someone like me. I need you to cover all my debts, past, present and future." At the cross Jesus not only wrote "Paid in full" across the record of our debts, he also tore up the ledger in which our debts could be written thereafter: "This he set aside, nailing it to the cross"

(Colossians 2:14). If you are in Christ, you are free and clear with God forever. Now you can make something of your life. That is where the sage goes next.

Opportunity

> Go to the ant, O sluggard;
>   consider her ways, and be wise.
> Without having any chief,
>   officer, or ruler,
> she prepares her bread in summer
>   and gathers her food in harvest.
> How long will you lie there, O sluggard?
>   When will you arise from your sleep?
> "A little sleep, a little slumber,
>   a little folding of the hands to rest,"[4]
> and your[5] poverty will come upon you like a robber,
>   and your want like an armed man. (Proverbs 6:6–11)

What is a sluggard? Think of the way syrup oozes slowly out of a bottle when it is cold. That is the sluggard—sluggish and slow and hesitant when he should be decisive, active, forthright. His life motto is, "Don't rush me." The Bible says, "As a door turns on its hinges, so does a sluggard on his bed" (Proverbs 26:14). He is lazy, constantly making the soft choice, losing one opportunity after another after another after another, day by day, moment by moment, until he lies there helpless in his wasted life. Let's all admit it— there is a sluggard deep inside each of us.

The sluggard reappears throughout the book of Proverbs.[6] What does Proverbs say about the sluggard? Three things. *First, the sluggard will not make up his mind.* There is a direct question in verse 9: "How long will you lie there? When will you arise from your sleep?" But that is too definite for the sluggard. He has no answer. He will not give an honest refusal, but he deceives himself by an endless sequence of little compromises.

Second, the sluggard will not finish things. On the rare occasions when he finds the motivation to get going, it is too much for him, and the impulse dies: "The sluggard buries his hand in the dish; it wears him out to bring it back to his mouth" (Proverbs 26:15). He does not stick with a task all the way through to a strong finish. He is a shallow person.

Third, the sluggard will not face things as they are. Rather than embrace the challenge of life, he dreams up excuses: "The sluggard says, 'There is a lion outside! I shall be killed in the streets!'" (Proverbs 22:13). A lion down on Main Street? I doubt it. What's really out there is a life, a job, a mission to fulfill for Christ.

What should the sluggard do? Go to the ant and take notes. How humiliating! The sluggard would not mind learning from John Calvin, maybe. The sluggard likes to debate and speculate and bandy highfalutin ideas around with his buddies. But wisdom is saying, "Go watch an ant!" I do not know anyone with a PhD in Antology. We all want to study big important things. And it is doubly humbling to go to ant school, because the Hebrew word for "ant" is in the feminine gender. But we guys need this, because we are too often passive. We are so accustomed to being wait-and-see, hang-back, and critical and guarded that we do not even feel the shame of it anymore. A church filled with men energized, men working, men engaged, men with intensity, men of conviction and action—that is exactly what the world needs to see in us today. But to display Christ that strongly, we need to humble ourselves and admit our need and accept God's simple remedy. It is so humbling that we, whom God created to rule over creation, need to go learn how to live from an ant. What then can we learn from an ant? Three things.[7]

First, inner motivation. Verse 7: "Without having any chief, officer, or ruler . . . " There is no Boss Ant standing over the others with a whip. Ants do not report in to anybody. No one has ever seen a foot-dragging ant. An ant has within herself all the motivation she needs to make something of her life, and she never lets up.

Second, hard work. Verse 8: "She prepares her bread in summer." Under that hot sun she scurries about and gets the job done. You are at a Fourth of July picnic, you are relaxing, but the ants are carrying off the sugar one grain at a time, and they will be back for the Fritos. I do not know if ants sweat, but if they do they do not care. They do not complain. They do not even wait. They are not above hard work and in fact seem to love it!

Third, future preparation. Verse 8: ". . . and gathers her food in harvest." The ant works today for tomorrow. She is not hoping life will go her way. She gets out ahead of the next season of life. Here is why that matters to you. There is a winter blast coming your way. I do not know when, I do not know how. And you do not need to go looking for it; it will come find you. But the winter of your discontent is coming. Are you getting ready, right now in this day of harvest? Are you stocking up on God's Word? Are you exploiting today as an opportunity from God to become wisely prepared for tomorrow? One year from today, are you going to be a more fruitful man of God? Well, *how* is that going to happen? What is your growth plan?

The gospel shows us such glory in God, and in ourselves because of Christ, that gospel-people become accomplishment-hungry. A Christian family should be like an anthill, everyone busily accomplishing something.

A healthy church is like an anthill, everybody actively achieving together. Wise people love goals and strategies to leverage their present into a better future. Sluggards are like Charles Dickens's Mr. Micawber, "waiting for something to turn up." *It won't.*

The sluggard procrastinates. He treats each precious moment of God-given life as no big deal. He is not astounded that the grace of God is giving him one more moment to live for Christ. What is the sluggard thinking? Verse 10: "'A little sleep, a little slumber, a little folding of the hands to rest.'" Just a little more, always just a little more. But "a little" is *not* a little. Verse 11 foresees the eventual cascade of consequences crashing into his life with inescapable force. There he is, a tragic buffoon, helpless and worthless. In his book *Lord, Make My Life a Miracle*, my dad concludes this way:

> Your danger and mine is not that we become criminals, but rather that we become respectable, decent, commonplace, mediocre Christians. The twentieth-century temptations that really sap our spiritual power are the television, banana cream pie, the easy chair, and the credit card. The Christian wins or loses in those seemingly innocent little moments of decision. Lord, make my life a miracle![8]

Maybe some of us have been settling for "a little," and not even noticing it. If so, how long will you lie there? When will you arise from your sleep and accomplish something great for Christ? Stop telling yourself you are a loser. Stop telling yourself your dad let you down. Stop making excuses. God has given you Christ, his very best. What are you going to do with your huge advantage, Jesus Christ?

As we get traction in this new way, we can expect counterattack. One of the devil's favorite strategies is to disrupt church unity:

Unity

A worthless person, a wicked man,
  goes about with crooked speech,
winks with his eyes, signals with his feet,
  points with his finger,
with perverted heart devises evil,
  continually sowing discord;
therefore calamity will come upon him suddenly;
  in a moment he will be broken beyond healing. (Proverbs 6:12–15)

The Bible looks at a sneaky, disruptive person and calls him "worthless" in verse 12. The Hebrew is *beliyyaᶜal*, meaning "without benefit or profit or use." That Hebrew word comes over into the New Testament as a name for the devil himself: "What accord has Christ with *Belial*?" (2 Corinthians 6:15). It is wonderful to have doubters and skeptics alongside believers in church. But in some churches in America today, we have members and even leaders who are not on Christ's side. Everyone sins stupidly. But some church people sin aggressively. That is what our passage condemns.

How do people sin aggressively? In little ways, but with huge impact. We see, in verse 13, the little acts of non-verbal communication—winking, signaling, pointing, all to sow discord. I remember sitting in the back row of a Christian meeting some years ago. The leader was up front. Then I noticed a man over at the right end of the back row leaning back in his seat, looking slyly at another man over on the left end of the back row, and rolling his eyes in disdain with a smirk on his face as if to say, "Can you believe that moron up front?" God is saying, in verse 15, "I will punish that behavior, because my Son died to bring you together in unity!" Look how intensely God feels about this:

> There are six things that the LORD hates,
>   seven that are an abomination to him:
> haughty eyes, a lying tongue,
>   and hands that shed innocent blood,
> a heart that devises wicked plans,
>   feet that make haste to run to evil,
> a false witness who breathes out lies,
>   and one who sows discord among brothers. (Proverbs 6:16–19)

When the Old Testament uses this literary device (x // x + 1), as in "three // four" (Proverbs 30:18–19, 29–31) or "six // seven," it is the last item in the list that matters most. The seventh thing the Lord hates, "one who sows discord among brothers," is the key to understanding the other six things the Lord hates. What he hates about haughty eyes is that their arrogance sows discord among brothers, what he hates about a lying tongue is how its gossip and slander sow discord among brothers, and so forth. God hates all discord *with a passion*. That's what "abomination" means. It turns his stomach.

But God delights in unity: "Behold, how good and pleasant it is when brothers dwell in unity!" (Psalm 133:1). Christ himself dwells in the midst of unity. Our unity is his cross becoming real in our hearts, as we demote Self for his sake and exalt him more. By our unity in Christ, we are not just being nice; we are being prophetic. We are saying to all the divisive, selfish idols of this world, "Jesus is Lord, *and you're not*. Jesus makes life sweet, *and you don't.* Jesus brings us together, *and you can't.* You have no claim on us here. We belong to the Lord Jesus Christ, the crucified Friend of sinners, and we will have the whole world know it by our strong and joyous unity in our Savior."

He who was in the form of God made himself nothing; he humbled himself down to our level, even down to the level of a servant, all the way down to the level of a condemned criminal. Therefore, God delighted to exalt him (Philippians 2:1–11). Okay, now we know how to live!

12

Why Our Sexuality Matters to God

PROVERBS 6:20—7:27

Can a man carry fire next to his chest
and his clothes not be burned?

6:27

THE SAGE AGAIN COUNSELS US about our sexuality. Why? Why does it matter that much to God? He is way up there, we are way down here. How much difference can our lives make to him? Augustine asked God, "What am I to you that you command me to love you, and that, if I fail to love you, you are angry with me and threaten me with vast miseries?"[1] Especially in our manhood and womanhood, such an earthy aspect of our existence, why does God care so much?

Our sexuality certainly matters to *us*, even intuitively. For example, when you are walking down the street, maybe going to the Post Office, and you happen to notice someone out of the corner of your eye, what is it about that person you notice first, without even thinking about it? Don't you notice whether that person is a man or a woman? And if you cannot tell, don't you take a second look? Or when you meet someone with a newborn baby, you ask, "Is it a boy or a girl?" Sexual identity matters to us. We know that our manhood or womanhood means something, it is worth something, it says something glorious. Think of all the songs and novels and poems and movies about romance. All of this matters to us, and it matters to God too.

Here is why. The gospel reveals something we never would have known. We are men and women playing out this drama of human romance over and over again because of who *God* is. Romance is not an evolution-generated mechanism for the survival of the human species. Romance came from God. Romance reveals God. Ultimate reality is not cold, dark, blank space out there going on forever with no meaning or message or emotion. Ultimate reality is romance. God loves us, and not with a platonic love but with a romantic love. God loves us not with chilly indifference but with hot passion. The gospel reveals that is who God is.

This wonderful truth means many things. For starters, it means marriage is not just another mutation in human social development. Marriage is a divine creation, pointing to something beyond us. A man and woman falling in love, committing themselves with lifelong vows of faithfulness, uniting sexually, living life together "'til death us do part"—it is all pointing to the mega-romance of Christ and the church in love forever. A man and a woman in love display the ultimate story of the Son of God coming down to win to his heart, with great suffering, a bride from the wrong side of town. God created the universe for the purpose of telling that love story. More than any other reason, *that* is why our sexuality matters, whether married or single. Just being a man is a gospel privilege. Just being a woman is a gospel privilege. What we are is about the gospel. That is why we need to learn gospel sexuality.

In Proverbs 6:20—7:27 the sage counsels his son about this massively significant area of life. The counsel is addressed to a son but applies equally to women. There are two major sections. In 6:20–35 the father warns us about the consequences of sexual folly. In 7:1–27 the father warns us about the strategies of sexual temptation. We will look at each section, and then we will turn to the New Testament to see the fuller relevance of it to us today— where we all can go for the love we crave.

The Consequences of Sexual Folly

> The commandment is a lamp and the teaching a light,
>   and the reproofs of discipline are the way of life,
> to preserve you from the evil woman,
>   from the smooth tongue of the adulteress.
> Do not desire her beauty in your heart,
>   and do not let her capture you with her eyelashes;
> for the price of a prostitute is only a loaf of bread,
>   but a married woman hunts down a precious life.
> Can a man carry fire next to his chest
>   and his clothes not be burned?

> Or can one walk on hot coals
>   and his feet not be scorched?
> So is he who goes in to his neighbor's wife;
>   none who touches her will go unpunished. (Proverbs 6:23–29)

Verses 20–35 work together to make one basic point—the high price of committing adultery. We need to be told, and we need to take it to heart: "Bind [this teaching] on your heart always" (v. 21). How then does wisdom counsel us, when we men notice a beautiful woman who is not our wife? Wisdom says, Don't even go there in your thoughts: "Do not desire her beauty in your heart" (v. 25). When a wise man sees a beautiful woman who is not his wife, here is how he thinks: "Yes, she is beautiful. *So?* Nothing to do with me. Beautiful *and irrelevant.* I am so out of here mentally!" And that wise man keeps going straight on ahead, for Christ, into a destiny of greatness. But a fool does not even have those categories.

If only evil were always ugly, life would be simpler. If only everything were color-coded to make it obvious, if only there were warning labels on all the poisons. But in this world disaster can be attractive. "Even Satan disguises himself as an angel of light" (2 Corinthians 11:14). He is magnificent. But does the magnificent devil know how to build a relationship? He seems so successful, but does he know how to live? The truth is, he is a fool, and he wants to make us his fools as we step on his well-concealed land mines.

The force of the argument here is real-life consequences. It is not primarily an ethical argument, a right-versus-wrong argument. It is a practical argument: ". . . the reproofs of discipline are the way of life" (v. 23)—not meaning what we mean by "way of life," that is, cultural norms, but rather the practical path *to life* (Psalm 16:11). If the sage were making his case with an ethical argument, he might arouse in us a nit-picky response about how far we can go before we cross a line into sin. Instead he helps us get right to the point. He tells us two things about the practical consequences of sexual folly.

First, the pain experienced is inevitable: "Can a man carry fire next to his chest and his clothes not be burned?" (v. 27). People who play with fire inevitably get burned. Fire can *only* burn. I have never heard anyone say to me, "Pastor, I committed adultery, and I'm so glad I did. My whole life has gotten better. That was the best decision I ever made." But I have heard people say, "If only I could relive that moment! If only I could go back and change what I did!" The pain is inevitable.

Second, the offense committed is unsatisfiable: "Jealousy makes a man furious, and he will not spare when he takes revenge" (v. 34). That is a realistic look at how an offended husband reacts when he finds out someone has had sex with his wife. If you are the offending man, do not expect forgiveness, expect revenge. I heard of a man in Dallas, a wealthy man, who committed adultery. The husband was furious, just as the Bible says. He told that man, "I'm going to kill you." So that wealthy man turned his home into a prison, with a fence all around and floodlights on his grounds at night and guard dogs.[2] An offended husband will not spare, because adultery attacks his home, his marriage, his honor, his manhood. If a man steals money to keep from starving, it is wrong but understandable (v. 30). But if a man steals another man's wife, if he sneaks into another man's personal sexual world, the Bible says that "his disgrace will not be wiped away" (v. 33). Even if that man repents and is restored to God through Christ, a memory in the family history will be, "Grandpa was the one who committed adultery."

That is the truth about sexual sin. It matters to God, and it matters to us. But is that the warning we hear from TV and the Internet and movies and magazines? No one but God levels with us. Several years ago a businessman was sent out of town by his company. The first night in the other city he phoned for a call girl. She came to his hotel room and knocked on the door. He opened the door, and there was his daughter. He immediately began having chest pains with an apparent heart attack.[3] Sexual folly carries consequences. They are inevitable and unsatisfiable. So we can praise God for being honest with us. He wants to help us walk in wisdom through the brothel of our modern world. And because every one of us is a sexual sinner at some level, here is how you can know right now where you stand with God:

> The difference between an unconverted man and a converted man is not that one has sins and the other has none; but that the one takes part with his cherished sins against a dreaded God, and the other takes part with a reconciled God against his hated sins.[4]

God wants to be your ally against your sins. Will you let him? Bring your sins to him and lay them at the foot of the cross. He promises to forgive you and to renew your broken life.

The Strategies of Sexual Temptation

My son, keep my words
  and treasure up my commandments with you;
keep my commandments and live;
    keep my teaching as the apple of your eye;
bind them on your fingers;
    write them on the tablet of your heart.
Say to wisdom, "You are my sister,"
  and call insight your intimate friend,

to keep you from the forbidden woman,
    from the adulteress with her smooth words. (Proverbs 7:1–5)

This is Old Testament language for what the New Testament calls being born again of the Holy Spirit (John 3:1–9). Something deep inside us changes. We start treasuring God's commands from the heart. We experience the gospel as an intimate friend. We are not ourselves geniuses. We are just saying to God's wisdom, "I want you more than I want any woman or man." Here is why we all need God to give us new hearts like that. Look at the kind of world we are living in:

For at the window of my house
    I have looked out through my lattice,
and I have seen among the simple,
    I have perceived among the youths,
    a young man lacking sense,
passing along the street near her corner,
    taking the road to her house
in the twilight, in the evening,
    at the time of night and darkness. (Proverbs 7:6–9)

The father saw something. He wants his teenage son to see it too, so he can walk into adulthood fully alert. The father tells us three things about the strategies of sexual temptation: the approach of temptation (vv. 6–13), the speech of temptation (vv. 14–20), and the impact of giving in to temptation (vv. 21–27).

Who is involved? The man, in this case, is one of "the simple." We have seen the simple before (Proverbs 1:4, 22). A simple person, a *petî*—related to the Hebrew verb meaning "to be open"—this person is keeping his options open, uncommitted, still "exploring life," we might say. So this particular simpleton is feeling restless early one evening and takes a walk. He is curious. He has heard about a certain part of town—or certain sites on the Internet. So there he goes, probably thinking, "I can handle this. I'm strong. And I need to see these things for myself anyway."

And behold, the woman meets him,
    dressed as a prostitute, wily of heart.
She is loud and wayward;
    her feet do not stay at home;
now in the street, now in the market,
    and at every corner she lies in wait. (Proverbs 7:10–12)

"Wily of heart" means, literally, "guarded of heart." She is unguarded in her dress, revealing much. But she is guarded in her heart, revealing nothing. There are men and women who do not know what a relationship is. They have never experienced it. They can role-play a relationship, but they do not give their hearts away. Sex they give, but themselves they guard. This young guy has no idea what he is walking into.

> She seizes him and kisses him,
>   and with bold face she says to him,
> "I had to offer sacrifices,
>   and today I have paid my vows;
> so now I have come out to meet you,
>   to seek you eagerly, and I have found you." (Proverbs 7:13–15)

Back in those times, religious sacrifices could include a meal from the meat of the animal sacrificed. Eating meat was a luxury anyway. So here the woman is saying, "Not only am I caught up on my religion, but I also have a feast of extra-special food waiting at home. It's a special occasion, like Prom Night or Mardi Gras. Come on, everybody needs a break. And you're the one I want to share all this with."

> "I have spread my couch with coverings,
>   colored linens from Egyptian linen;
> I have perfumed my bed with myrrh,
>   aloes, and cinnamon." (Proverbs 7:16, 17)

Only the rich owned furniture in their homes back in this world. So this guy thinks he is hitting the jackpot. A beautiful woman, a great feast, a luxurious setting, exotic experiences are all just waiting for him.

> "Come, let us take our fill of love till morning;
>   let us delight ourselves with love." (Proverbs 7:18)

The Hebrew here could be paraphrased and expanded, "Come, let's saturate ourselves with love-making in all its forms; let's enjoy ourselves with every act, all night long, slowly passing the night, no hurry." But as one commentator points out,

> To have a full sexual relationship with somebody is to give physical expression to what is meant to be a covenanted relationship—that is, stable, faithful, permanent. To say physically, "I am giving myself to you," while emotionally and spiritually holding back from covenanted commitment is in fact to live a lie—a split in the personality which is ultimately stressful and destructive.[5]

"For my husband is not at home;
    he has gone on a long journey;
he took a bag of money with him;
    at full moon he will come home." (Proverbs 7:19, 20)

"Nobody will ever know" is the temptation. But if she is willing to betray her husband, why does Mr. Dimwit think she will be fair to him? The offer of sin-with-no-regret is how Satan lied to us in the Garden of Eden. When (not if) a man or woman tempts you with the assurance that no one will ever know, that person is really saying to you, "God does not exist."

But this young man, on an impulse, falls for the temptation: "All at once he follows her, as an ox goes to the slaughter" (v. 22). Why like a dumb ox? Because "the wages of sin is death" (Romans 6:23). They just are. We cannot change that by any amount of wishful thinking. We must not think, "What happens down in Mexico stays in Mexico." It doesn't. But by the time this young man feels the impact, it will be too late.

He is not the only one. History is like a battlefield, with casualties of sexual folly lying everywhere: "Many a victim has she laid low, and all her slain are a mighty throng" (v. 26). It is no accident that Babylon's most important female deity, Ishtar, was the goddess of love and war,[6] because in this world of folly, sex and violence have long gone together. But Ishtar is a powerful goddess. In our modern world, studies now show that pornography rewires our brains with addictive power, taking us prisoner.[7] But we can be wired back for intimacy with God and real relationships with others through God's redeeming love.

It is not enough for us to know how foolish we have been. We also need to know how good it is really to be loved. Maybe you have noticed that something is missing from this entire passage here in Proverbs. The word "God" appears nowhere in this text. But elsewhere in the Bible we find out how good it is to be loved by God.

Where to Find the Love We Long For

Do you not know that your bodies are members of Christ? Shall I then take the members of Christ and make them members of a prostitute? Never! Or do you not know that he who is joined to a prostitute becomes one body with her? For, as it is written, "The two will become one flesh." But he who is joined to the Lord becomes one spirit with him. (1 Corinthians 6:15–17)

The concept of "accepting Jesus" is Biblical (John 1:12), but it is often misunderstood. In America's Bible Belt especially, many people need to be saved from their salvation. They have "accepted Jesus" in the sense that they have allowed him into their lives, up to a point. But this passage in 1 Corinthians 6 shows us more. Becoming a Christian is the joining of two into one. It is trust and surrender such that we give ourselves entirely to Christ, like sexual union. But if all you have done is "accept Jesus" on your terms so that you retain control of your life, you have only flirted with Christ. You need to go all the way. Then you will feel loved.

Here is what it means to be a Christian. You become joined to the Lord Jesus Christ, in body and spirit, through his finished work on the cross. He gives himself to you completely by grace, and you give yourself to him completely by faith. Not only your spirit but also the members of your body, your very organs, are so indwelt by the living Christ that you are his physical presence in the world today. From head to toe, all that you are is not only *for* Christ but also *of* Christ. That includes your sexuality, married or single, because you *are* married—to Christ. You have been joined by grace to the Lord. You have been brought into union with the most loving Person in the universe. He is giving his love to you with all his passionate heart. He is so close to you, he identifies so intensely with you, the Bible is saying he and you have become one spirit, the way a married man and woman become one flesh. But to be one spirit is even more profound, more intimate, deeper, and richer than to be one flesh. And Paul wrote this to *sinful* Christians. Throughout the New Testament this Corinthian church was the biggest mess of all. But Christ loves and redeems people no one else can love. He loves *you* to this full extent.

Will you believe it, receive it, and open your heart to Christ today?

13

The Worldview of Wisdom

PROVERBS 8:1–36

I was daily filled with delight,
rejoicing before him always,
rejoicing in his inhabited world
and delighting in the children of man.[1]

8:30, 31

IN PROVERBS 7 GOD TELLS US not to commit adultery. Now in chapter 8 God lifts before us a brightly positive worldview. So here we find these two things side-by-side: sex—worldview. God is giving us coping strategies for moments of temptation. But he is also giving us a whole new way of see-ing *everything*. We naturally tend to think piecemeal. But the God-centered wholeness of life is wisdom, and it is joyous. That is what Proverbs 8 is about, the joyous grandeur of Christ, relevant to all of life, with higher aims and richer rewards than we would otherwise even contemplate.

The sage is teaching us the doctrine of creation. If we split our thinking between a small area called "religion" over here on Sunday, while the rest of life called "the real me" is over there Monday through Saturday, we diminish Jesus to the level of Jesus Jr. But all of life comes from the wise and gener-ous hand of our glorious Creator-Savior.

The doctrine of creation runs throughout the Bible. Genesis 1:1: "In the beginning, God created the heavens and the earth." Revelation 4:11: "Worthy are you, our Lord and God, to receive glory and honor and power, for you created all things." Living in his universe, we have nothing to fear and everything to enjoy. God made it all, for us, to the praise of his glory. So there goes superstition. There goes asceticism. There goes stoicism. There goes religious grumpiness. The doctrine of creation makes human life sweet and significant.

But if the doctrine of creation is true, and it is, then why do we all resonate with T. S. Eliot's description of modern culture as "shape without form, shade without color, paralyzed force, gesture without motion"?[1] Why do our own lives spiral down into contradiction, frustration, and just plain boredom? Here is why. We take our favorite aspect of the creation, and we make it into an idol. We pin our hopes on some good thing that lets us down because it cannot bear us up. We fixate on family or money or success or ministry with an excessive emotional expectation. Then when it leaves us empty, we fall into despair. We can even project our personal despair onto the cosmos philosophically, as if reality itself were mocking our hearts.[2] So God mercifully steps in with the wise doctrine of creation. It frees us from our idols. It exalts Christ. It makes life livable again.

Proverbs 8 is that wisdom. It divides into four sections. Wisdom commands us to prize her (vv. 1–11). Why prize wisdom? Because she is both powerful (vv. 12–21) and profound (vv. 22–31). Wisdom is the real power behind the throne, enriching all who love her (verses 12–21). And wisdom is the secret to the universe: she was here first, rejoicing over God's creation (vv. 22–31). Finally, wisdom is the *one* necessity for true life, and we *must* embrace her (vv. 32–36).

Throughout Proverbs 8 the sage is speaking. But he uses a figure of speech called personification. As he writes, he takes on the persona of Wisdom as an elegant lady. I think of her as Galadriel, the elf queen, in The Lord of the Rings books and movies—lovely, dignified, wise. She is the opposite of the adulteress in Proverbs 7. But because this is in the Bible, the ultimate voice we are hearing here is Christ himself.

Wisdom Calls and Commands
> Does not wisdom call?
>> Does not understanding raise her voice?
> On the heights beside the way,
>> at the crossroads she takes her stand;
> beside the gates in front of the town,
>> at the entrance of the portals she cries aloud . . . (Proverbs 8:1–3)

Christ does not retreat into a monastery. He does not wait for us to find him. He moves toward us, he moves toward the masses, where we live day by day, "at the crossroads," where the competition for hearts is fiercest. He rubs shoulders with us. He feels at home with us. He speaks into our everyday lives. But he is *not* whispering "softly and tenderly," as the old hymn puts it. He is raising his voice, so that we can hear him above all the noise. There is no question about his relevance to us or his interest in us. The only question is, are we listening? Are we turning the noise down so that we *can* listen?

To whom does Christ make his appeal? Not to scholars, not even to religious people. His heart is bigger than that:

> To you, O men, I call,
>   and my cry is to the children of man.
> O simple ones, learn prudence;
>   O fools, learn sense. (Proverbs 8:4, 5)

Jesus Christ wants to engage everyone, including fools who have made many mistakes. There is one group he does ignore: the scoffers. "Whoever corrects a scoffer gets himself abuse" (Proverbs 9:7). Some people just will not listen. If you try to help them, they get mean. But as for the rest of us—even if we are fools, Christ is reaching out to us. All he asks is humble openness. He provides everything else. Look at what he is offering us:

> Hear, for I will speak noble things,
>   and from my lips will come what is right,
> for my mouth will utter truth;
>   wickedness is an abomination to my lips.
> All the words of my mouth are righteous;
>   there is nothing twisted or crooked in them.
> They are all straight to him who understands,
>   and right to those who find knowledge. (Proverbs 8:6–9)

Christ gives us two commands in verses 1–11. The first is in verse 6: "Hear." Why should we listen with complete openness? Because all the words of his mouth are righteous—completely true and morally excellent. There is nothing hidden or tricky or manipulative in the Bible. *God has never said anything he had to be ashamed of or take back.* The problem for us is, he is willing to tell us hard things. He does not flatter us. He can be blunt. So we have to decide if we are going to listen enough so that we change. But Christ is incapable of giving us less than noble things. Do you see the word "noble" in verse 6? There is nothing degrading in the gospel. His gospel raises our standards and lifts us above the vulgar. In our sloppy modern culture of self-indulgence, that helps. Sometimes his words come with a bite, and we have to swallow hard, but there is no bitter aftertaste.

Here is the catch. Verse 9: "They are all straight *to him who understands*, and right *to those who find knowledge*." That is to say, the Word of God is open to the open person, it is reasonable to the reasonable person. You must understand this about yourself. How you experience the Word of God reveals *yourself* to you (2 Corinthians 2:14–16). If your own mentality, your own interior world, is biased in favor of Self, the gospel will leave you feeling misunderstood and underappreciated, and you will resent it, and you will blame the gospel or at least the preacher of the gospel. You might even lash back. This is why every one of us must bring to our every encounter with the gospel a certain pre-condition. We must come pre-committed humbly to obey whatever Christ says. The Bible says, "Receive with meekness the implanted word, which is able to save your souls" (James 1:21). How could it be otherwise? Christ will not allow us to treat him as a theory, at intellectual arm's length. But if you are hungry for him, he will give you his very best, *as you listen.*

That is the Lord's first command—to hear. The second of the two commands in verses 1–11 appears in verse 10:

> Take my instruction instead of silver,
>   and knowledge rather than choice gold,
> for wisdom is better than jewels,
>   and all that you may desire cannot compare with her. (Proverbs 8:10, 11)

See the word "take"? We have to choose what we are going to take and grab hold of and not let go. We cannot have it all: "Take my instruction *instead of* silver." It is an either/or choice, because whatever we take takes us. We will love either wisdom or money. We will most deeply care about what we are or what we have. We cannot live for two ultimate goals at once (Matthew 6:24). Make your money serve Christ, or you will end up serving it without Christ.

Why choose his wisdom rather than money? Verses 12–31 tell us why. Verses 12–21 exult in wisdom's broad relevance to life now, and verses 22–31 exult in wisdom's deep antiquity before life now.

Wisdom Rules and Enriches

> I, wisdom, dwell with prudence,
>   and I find knowledge and discretion.
> The fear of the LORD is hatred of evil.
>   Pride and arrogance and the way of evil
>   and perverted speech I hate.
> I have counsel and sound wisdom;
>   I have insight; I have strength. (Proverbs 8:12–14)

We take whatever we value. And Christ, speaking as Wisdom, is saying here that the people he blesses join him in fearing the Lord and hating pride and self-importance and sneakiness (v. 13), which are the very sins to which gifted people are prone. But wisdom has the patent on counsel and resourcefulness and insight and heroic strength (v. 14). Wisdom provides both strategies that succeed and the strength to carry them out and not quit in the face of hardship and opposition. Wisdom is practical. Wisdom works. Wisdom makes us influential. But the wisdom of Christ belongs only to those who humble themselves, because they want to change and grow and make an impact for him.

This is not natural wisdom. This is spiritual wisdom. There is a difference (James 3:13–18). For example, the hero of the Babylonian account of the flood is a man named Utnapishtim.[3] He was even given another name meaning something like "Super-Genius." He was brilliant. By contrast, the Bible says that Noah was "righteous" and "walked with God" (Genesis 6:9; 7:1). But who was really smart? Mr. Super-Genius or the believer who walked humbly with God? Utnapishtim built his boat as a giant cube, 180 feet in length, width, and height, with a displacement of over 200,000 tons. It would have sunk to the bottom like a stone. Noah built something like a modern battleship, 450 feet long, seventy-five feet wide, forty-five feet high, with a displacement of around 43,300 tons—a sensible plan.[4] The Bible never says Noah was brilliant. But he did walk with God. And guess what? It worked out for him. It will work out for you too.

> By me kings reign,
>   and rulers decree what is just;
> by me princes rule,
>   and nobles, all who govern justly. (Proverbs 8:15, 16)

Even in the tough world of human leadership, Christ is the secret to success. He knows his way around hardheaded deals and aggressive negotiations. He knows how to get things done with agility, versatility, keenness, competence. Oh, how we underrate his abilities and resources when everything is on the line! And for a church, success does not require human rules. Rules do not make people thrive. Success requires wise, seasoned, humble, mature, Christlike leaders. And in Christ you can become one of them. He is generous with himself:

> I love those who love me,
>   and those who seek me diligently find me.
> Riches and honor are with me,
>   enduring wealth and righteousness.

> My fruit is better than gold, even fine gold,
>   and my yield than choice silver.
> I walk in the way of righteousness,
>   in the paths of justice,
> granting an inheritance to those who love me,
>   and filling their treasuries. (Proverbs 8:17–21)

We are hearing here the language of love. Christ is promising us his fullness, from his very heart. We cannot come up empty-handed, if we seek him with a diligent heart. "Those who seek me diligently find me" (verse 17)—that adverb "diligently" means "with intentionality, going out of our usual way, breaking with routine." God honors an earnest heart. He even offers a seeker "riches and honor" (v. 18). He does not despise earthly incentives. To gain a precious treasure, full of meaning and symbolic of his favor, is despised only by cranks and killjoys. If we love and seek money as our prize, it will ruin us. The Bible warns us that just desiring money—not necessarily getting it but just *desiring* it—destroys us (1 Timothy 6:9). But if we love and seek Christ as the prize of our hearts, he supplies all the money and all the treasure and all the honor we will need to love him and serve him according to his will and plan for us.[5] And that kind of gracious privilege cannot ruin us, because it doesn't own us deep inside. Jesus does.

You might be thinking, "Nice concept. But I'm not that spiritual. I guess I'm excluded." Look what Christ says in verse 20: "I walk in the way of righteousness." Do you see? If he walks in the way of righteousness, how can he fail to keep his promises even to fools and beginners who are seeking him? He loves not geniuses and experts—he loves those who love him. Just love him enough to seek him.

Verses 12–21 give us reasons to hear and take the wisdom of Christ rather than everything this fraudulent world offers. Verses 22–31 go all the way back to the beginning, back to the creation, with more reasons to hear and take his wisdom:

Wisdom Preceded and Celebrated

> The LORD possessed me at the beginning of his work,
>   the first of his acts of old.
> Ages ago I was set up,
>   at the first, before the beginning of the earth.
> When there were no depths I was brought forth,
>   when there were no springs abounding with water.
> Before the mountains had been shaped,
>   before the hills, I was brought forth,
> before he had made the earth with its fields,

or the first of the dust of the world.
When he established the heavens, I was there;
    when he drew a circle on the face of the deep,
when he made firm the skies above,
    when he established the fountains of the deep,
when he assigned to the sea its limit,
    so that the waters might not transgress his command,
when he marked out the foundations of the earth,
    then I was beside him, like a master workman,[6]
and I was daily filled with delight,[7]
    rejoicing before him always,
rejoicing in his inhabited world
    and delighting in the children of man. (Proverbs 8:22–31)

Now Proverbs 8 rises to a glorious crescendo over *the profound happiness of wisdom*. What is the paragraph saying? Wisdom was here first, before us. Wisdom was God's first creation. He wired wisdom into the cosmos as the inner logic of everything. So wisdom was how everything started and how everything still works. We are born into this world long after things were set up so amazingly. What do we know? We cannot control our environment; we adjust to it. So Biblical wisdom is more than handy tips. Wisdom is the secret code to reality. And in the Bible it is speaking to us, so that it isn't a secret anymore.

What is the sage's point in writing this? Two things. First, wisdom is external to us. The wisdom we need for our lives is not inside us; it is outside us. There is a reason why we have ears on the *outside* of our heads. We are not meant to listen to ourselves. We have too much to learn. Even God himself did nothing without wisdom. How can *we* do anything without it? And we have a good reason to listen to Christ's wisdom. Here is the reason.

Second, wisdom is joyous over us. Wisdom is not a nag. Joy breaks out whenever wisdom is exercised. Verses 24–26 describe the pre-creation conditions that God shaped into the creation. Wisdom is saying, "When everything was still a chaotic mess, without form and void, God created me first to fix it. God considered me indispensable. So how about your life? Could I help you with your mess?" And the one offering herself—but really, this is Christ speaking—the one offering himself is *joyous* about his creation. Christ is enthusiastic about his creation, he is exuberant, he is wholehearted. You have every reason to turn your life over to him and say, "Re-create me."

Here is the gospel. Because of God, everything in the creation is good. Because of Adam, everything God made is marred and tragic—including our personal responses to everything God made. Because of Christ, everything God made will be redeemed. So even now everything is, in principle, eligible for wise enjoyment under Christ (1 Timothy 4:1–5). The NFL is good, fallen, and redeemable. Gardening is good, fallen, and redeemable. Your job is good, fallen, and redeemable. Everything—the arts, the military, family life—everything God created is good, and we should *rejoice* in God our Creator. John Calvin was believing the doctrine of creation when he wrote, "There is not one little blade of grass, there is no color in this world, that is not intended to make men rejoice."[8] The doctrine of creation has gospel power to put life and zest back into us:

Rev. Theodore L. Cuyler, the celebrated Brooklyn divine, was visiting the famous London preacher Rev. Charles H. Spurgeon. After a hard day of work and serious discussion, these two mighty men of God went out into the country together for a holiday. They roamed the fields in high spirits like boys let loose from school, chatting and laughing and free from care. Dr. Cuyler had just told a story at which Mr. Spurgeon laughed uproariously. Then suddenly he turned to Dr. Cuyler and exclaimed, "Theodore, let's kneel down and thank God for laughter!" And there, on the green carpet of grass, under the trees, two of the world's greatest men knelt and thanked the dear Lord for the bright and joyous gift of laughter.[9]

Only the Biblical worldview gushes with enthusiasm over this world we live in and our own humanness. It frees us to enthuse. The Bible says, "A joyful heart is good medicine" (Proverbs 17:22). Here is how we guard it and deepen it, for the glory of God.

Wisdom Invites and Warns

"And now, O sons, listen to me:
  blessed are those who keep my ways.
Hear instruction and be wise,
  and do not neglect it.
Blessed is the one who listens to me,
  watching daily at my gates,
  waiting beside my doors.
For whoever finds me finds life
  and obtains favor from the LORD,
but he who fails to find me injures himself;
  all who hate me love death." (Proverbs 8:32–36)

The wisdom of Christ is the one and only true necessity in your life. And you must embrace him wholeheartedly. You must become decisive for him. "Wisdom is possible for man by following, by discipleship,"[10] not by holding back in critical detachment with an endless wait-and-see skepticism. But if you do enter in, Christ is promising you a true life, a life worth living, under the smile of God. Hold everything else lightly, but grab hold of Jesus Christ, the crucified Friend of sinners and never let him go. "Whoever has the Son has life; whoever does not have the Son of God does not have life" (1 John 5:12).

The irony is, if you protect yourself from him, you injure yourself. Verse 36 could be translated, "He who fails to find me does *violence* to himself." Christ loves you more than you love yourself. And you can have him, not by heroic intellectual pursuit but by humbly admitting the truth—you are a fool who needs a Sage. If you are a fool, you are the one he loves. Will you listen and take him? He promises you everything you desire in your own deepest intentions.

14

It's Decision Time

PROVERBS 9:1–18

"Whoever is simple, let him turn in here!"

9:4

AS WE COME TO PROVERBS 9, we are confronted with a choice. The passage portrays two houses, one on either side of the road. On one side, a house stands open, with an elegant lady named Wisdom inviting us in. On the other side of the road, another house stands open, with a seductive lady named Folly inviting us in. Which way will we turn?

The "right" answer is easy—in theory. We are often told today that all we need is the right information. If we will do the research on the Internet we will know what to do next. But in reality we are running back and forth between these two houses all the time. The right choice is obvious, but we ourselves are complicated. So, before we jump into Proverbs 9, we need to understand two things.

First, we have histories. We are no longer blank slates. We have scribbles and erasures and misspellings and doodlings written messily all over us. In fact, we were *born* complicated. We were born with a bias toward folly. We were born guilty. Theologians call it Original Sin, and it is real. It explains why our wills are unfree. It explains why even obvious choices can be difficult or impossible. Our hearts are corrupt down beneath the level of choice. So, just knowing the right thing to do is not always enough. Indeed, our problem is still worse. Add onto our underlying depravity the layers of scar tissue, so to speak, from the sins we have committed and the wounds we have suffered, including scar tissue from botched surgeries, mostly self-performed. All of that complication is the real you and the real me poised here at the crossroads of Proverbs 9. That is the unsimple you and me for whom an obvious choice can be paralyzing. But that is the real you and me God loves and understands and wants to help.

Second, in the gospel God addresses the real us in a new way. We have already seen this in Proverbs. The word "son" (or "sons") appears twenty-two times in Proverbs 1—8. That word from God tells you who you are now in Christ. That word of grace opens up your future. It makes the wise choice here in chapter 9 not only possible but joyous. Again and again God looks you in the eye and calls you his beloved, in whom he is well-pleased, for the sake of Christ. The Bible says, "God is treating you as sons" (Hebrews 12:7), not as losers. The Bible says Christ is not ashamed to call us his brothers (Hebrews 2:11). The Bible says, "And stretching out his hand toward his disciples, Jesus said, 'Here are . . . my brothers!'" (Matthew 12:49). How can you define yourself out as a reject when God has already defined you in as a child, and therefore an heir of every promise he has ever made? William Romaine, the Anglican pastor during the Great Awakening, taught us how to see ourselves in a new gospel way: "Consider your state. You are a pardoned sinner, not under the law but under grace, freely, fully saved from the guilt of all your sins. There is none to condemn, God having justified you. He sees you in his Son, washed you in his blood, clothed you in his righteousness, and he embraces him and you, the head and the members, with the same affection."[1] Christ has come to the real us to say, "I'm changing the subject from your failure, your impasse, your defeatedness to my grace!" We are humbled, we are encouraged, and now we are ready for Proverbs 9.

The passage divides into three paragraphs of six verses each. The first and third paragraphs mirror one another like bookends, each one with an invitation. The sage is telling us, "It's an either/or decision. There is no third option." The invitation to wisdom stands open to everyone—with one exception. Scoffers are excluded (vv. 7, 12). The middle paragraph in chapter 9 explains why God ignores scoffers. But he welcomes both the wise and the simple.

Wisdom's Invitation to Life

> Wisdom has built her house;
> > she has hewn her seven pillars. (Proverbs 9:1)

Wisdom is personified as a classy lady, opening to us her palatial home. But what is the sage talking about in real terms? Taking the whole Bible into account, this is a picture of Jesus Christ as a wealthy and wise Friend who has thought of everything we need and provided it in full. The word for "wisdom" here in verse 1 is singular in English but plural in the Hebrew—"wisdoms." It isn't a numerical plural, it isn't alternative wisdoms to choose from; it is a plural of majesty[2] for wisdom in all its perfections and fullness. Jesus Christ lacks nothing we need. Here is another Biblical way of saying it: "My soul will be satisfied as with fat and rich food" (Psalm 63:5). Jesus himself said, "I came that they may have life and have it abundantly" (John 10:10). The fact that Wisdom's house has "seven pillars" says the same thing—effort in hewing them out, wealth to finance them (ordinary homes did not have pillars), and perfection in completing them. If you think of Jesus as a really nice but incompetent person, a religious idealist for people whose lives are sufficiently privileged that they can afford that luxury, you do not understand him at all. He is the greatest expert in the universe on you, and he is better at building a great life for you than you are.

> She has slaughtered her beasts; she has mixed her wine;
> she has also set her table. (Proverbs 9:2)

No junk food at this feast! Lady Wisdom has been bustling about preparing a banquet of her best—for us. Mixing the wine does not mean watering it down. It means adding in spices to make the wine even better. The point of verse 2 is, what Christ offers you is ready right now, and it couldn't be more loving or generous or honoring to you.

But again, what is the reality behind the metaphor? Let's think back over what we have learned thus far in the book of Proverbs. This table spread with wisdom has delicacies to satisfy us in every area of life. Proverbs chapter 1—wisdom preserves us from violent people. Chapter 2—wisdom enters our hearts with peace of conscience. Chapter 3—wisdom improves us financially. Chapter 4—wisdom elevates our status in society. Chapter 5—wisdom makes sex better. Chapter 6—wisdom gets us up off the sofa and successfully accomplishing worthy goals. Chapter 7—wisdom protects us in temptation. Chapter 8—wisdom opens our eyes to the joyous creation in which we live. And that's just for starters. We have not even gotten to the actual proverbs yet, in chapters 10—31. Christ has set a good table for us.

> She has sent out her young women to call
> from the highest places in the town,
> "Whoever is simple, let him turn in here!"
> To him who lacks sense she says,
> "Come, eat of my bread
> and drink of the wine I have mixed.

Leave the company of the simple,[3] and live,
    and walk in the way of insight." (Proverbs 9:3–6)

Wisdom—really, Christ himself—has sent messengers out into the world to invite more and more people into his banquet. Wisdom is bold and public. Wisdom cares deeply about people. And we are his messengers today. But even though we are involved, a divine voice is being heard. A more literal translation of verse 3 is, "She has sent out her young women, she calls . . . " That is, her servants are getting the invitations out, but Lady Wisdom herself is speaking through them. It is a picture of the prophets and the apostles. It is a picture of Christian parents and Sunday school teachers and preachers today. The Bible says, "When you received the word of God, which you heard from us, you accepted it not as the word of men but as . . . the word of God" (1 Thessalonians 2:13). This understanding of the ministry of the gospel is almost forgotten today. When I am preaching, I am not tossing out my own opinions. *I* don't even care about my opinions. Why should you? But previous generations understood and revered and enjoyed what is really happening in the preaching moment. The Second Helvetic Confession of 1566 says, "The preaching of the Word of God is the Word of God."[4] When you can see in your Bible that what the preacher is saying comes from the Bible, you are hearing the Word of God. God is inviting you into the banquet. The preacher's job is not to complicate it; your job is to receive it. God is inviting us all into joys we have never known before, because they come down from Heaven.

Anyone can join the party: "Whoever is simple, let him turn in here!" Remember that "the simple" is the beginner who lacks commitment. But Christ is so humble to welcome us in, just as we are. Here is a simple gospel mantra always to keep in mind: "One, I am a complete idiot. Two, my future is incredibly bright. Three, anyone can get in on this." All we have to do is turn to him: "Whoever is simple, let him turn in here!" That is repentance. Gospel repentance is more than turning away from sin. Gospel repentance is, first and foremost, turning toward Jesus Christ. How can you and I ever turn completely from our sins anyway? As the old hymn says, "If you tarry till you're better, you will never come at all." Christ is inviting us to come now to receive his very best: "Come, eat of my bread and drink of the wine I have mixed" (v. 5). He is telling us to come freely and eat fully. Dietrich Bonhoeffer, in *The Cost of Discipleship*, wrote against what he called "cheap grace."[5] He had a point. But be careful. Grace must be cheap or it isn't grace anymore. It wasn't cheap to Christ at the cross, but it is cheap to us. That is exactly the force of verses 4, 5: a fine banquet of grace, freely open to fools.

Here is the price we do pay: "Leave the company of the simple" (v. 6). Why is that there? Because Christ is creating a new *community* of wisdom. He is so wise. Here is what he understands about us. To some degree our reality is socially constructed, music being an obvious example. Music brings people together, but it also drives people apart. Parents cannot understand why their kids love that noise in the iPod, but that same music ties the kids closely to their peers. Music divides up according to the generations, their corporate memory, the soundtrack of their lives. Even so, when Christ brings us to himself, we enter a new group experience. Community in Christ isn't a legalistic rule against missing church; it is plugging into the power of sharing Christ together. Your old group cannot give you that. You should keep on loving them. But you have a new community in Christ, where you *can* "walk in the way of insight."

Why Scoffers Are Excluded

> Whoever corrects a scoffer gets himself abuse,
>   and he who reproves a wicked man incurs injury.
> Do not reprove a scoffer, or he will hate you;
>   reprove a wise man, and he will love you.
> Give instruction to a wise man, and he will be still wiser;
>   teach a righteous man, and he will increase in learning.
> The fear of the LORD is the beginning of wisdom,
>   and the knowledge of the Holy One is insight.
> For by me your days will be multiplied,
>   and years will be added to your life.
> If you are wise, you are wise for yourself;
>   if you scoff, you alone will bear it. (Proverbs 9:7–12)

Every one of us needs someone to whom we regularly say, "How can I improve?" And then we need to listen. Openness and humility are how we grow. Scoffers are not like that. What is a "scoffer"? A scoffer is anyone who never accepts correction. He thinks other people really need his opinions. He is easily offended. He is above other people. And if someone seems to threaten his superiority, he scoffs. He mocks. He mouths off. He denigrates.

> No man earns more universal detestation or deserves it more than he who wears a perpetual sneer, who is himself incapable of deep loyalty and reverence and who supposes that it is his mission in life to promote the corrosion of the values by which individuals and society live. He is the person with the knowing wink and the clever phrase who has seen through the hollowness of everything.[6]

This kind of person is dangerous. If you cross him, he will punish you—

and claim it is your fault. We see it in the strife abounding in our churches today. It is the mood of our culture. Why? What has happened to us? Paul Vischer, creator of VeggieTales, spoke at Yale in 2005 and explained it this way:

> For me and for many others in my generation, the real root [of our cynicism] is . . . personal. When we were very young, our parents broke their promises. Their promises to each other, and their promises to us. And millions of American kids in a very short period of time learned that the world isn't a safe place; that there isn't anyone who won't let you down; that their hearts were much too fragile to leave exposed. And sarcasm, as C. S. Lewis put it, "builds up around a man the finest armor-plating . . . that I know."[7]

We have all been let down. And by now we have no reason not to be cynical scoffers—no reason except Jesus. And he is reason enough. He will never let us down. He is why we humble ourselves and open up and listen. He is why the tone of our churches need not be sarcasm but reverence: "The fear of the LORD is the beginning of wisdom, and the knowledge of the Holy One is insight" (v. 10). We revere Jesus as the Holy One, which means he is outside our categories, surprising us, especially as he loves us more than we love him. The truth is, we have let him down so many times. But here is his heart toward us: "I will not execute my burning anger . . . for I am God and not man, the Holy One in your midst" (Hosea 11:9). The Holy One is sweet-natured. He is the easiest person in the universe to get along with. He did say, "Those whom I love, I reprove and discipline" (Revelation 3:19) But because it is his loving heart speaking into our lives, we open up and say, "Lord, I *want* to know how I can grow. Please tell me." That humble eagerness is wisdom. It is the fear of the Lord. It is reverence.

Revering him makes all the difference for every one of us in the most personal way: "If you are wise, you are wise for yourself; if you scoff, you alone will bear it" (v. 12). As important as community is, I cannot borrow character from you, nor can you borrow character from me. Just being at church will not change us. No one gets a degree from Vanderbilt by hanging out on campus and blending in with the students. Even so, each of us must receive Christ personally. We must seek him and engage with him personally. *He* is how we change. *He* is how wisdom enters into us. And when he gives it to us, no one can take it away from us, no matter what they say or do. Are we laying hold of Christ? Are we saying in our hearts, "I refuse to read the great stories of how God has blessed others in the past and just leave it there. This is my moment. This is my life. And I need Christ now. I will not let him go until he blesses me"? He loves to answer that prayer. Good thing, given the world we are walking through.

Folly's Invitation to Death

> The woman Folly is loud;
>> she is seductive and knows nothing.
> She sits at the door of her house;
>> she takes a seat on the highest places of the town,
> calling to those who pass by,
>> who are going straight on their way,
> "Whoever is simple, let him turn in here!"
>> And to him who lacks sense she says,
> "Stolen water is sweet,
>> and bread eaten in secret is pleasant."
> But he does not know that the dead are there,
>> that her guests are in the depths of Sheol. (Proverbs 9:13–18)

That is a picture of our world today. In the Revelation of John our two great enemies are the Beast and the Prostitute—the Beast to savage us, and the Prostitute to seduce us. Here in the West, the Prostitute is our primary threat. She is soft and soothing, but just as destructive as the Beast. That is not always easy for us to see. Here in verses 13–18 the parallels with Wisdom's invitation in verses 1–6 are striking. The message is even the same: "Whoever is simple, let him turn in here!" (vv. 4, 16). But there are differences. First, Wisdom builds her house, but Folly just sits there and expects us to be impressed. Second, Wisdom offers us meat and wine, but Folly offers us bread and water. Third, Wisdom is dealing honestly with us, but Folly is making glamorous promises that cannot come true. Fourth, Wisdom's followers live more and more forever, but Folly's playmates die a sugarcoated death before they even know what hit them.

Folly is truthful at one point. Stolen water *is* sweet to us—for a little while, that is, until the guilt sets in. But our corrupt hearts have a relish for evil. Augustine was honest about himself. In his autobiography he told about a moment of self-discovery when he stole something he already had plenty of. He stole *because* it was wrong, because doing something wrong and getting away with it was exciting. And Augustine wrote, "Such was my heart, O God, such was my heart. You had pity on it when it was at the bottom of the abyss."[8]

Do you have a taste for sin, vulgarity, and folly? We all do. We all know what it is like to be stuck down there in that abyss of Self where we cannot even choose Christ. What do we do then? How can we choose him as the passion of our lives when we are passionate for lesser things, even wrong things? How can we jump out of a hole that has no bottom? There is only one way. We hear the gospel again. Jesus Christ loves you—not the rehabilitated you but the real you down in that abyss—and he welcomes you to himself. Charles Haddon Spurgeon helped us see the grace of Christ more clearly when he said,

> The gate of Mercy is opened, and over the door it is written, "This is a faithful saying and worthy of all acceptation, that Christ Jesus came into the world to save *sinners.*" Between that word "save" and the next word "sinners," there is no adjective. It does not say, "penitent sinners," "awakened sinners," "sensible sinners," "grieving sinners," or "alarmed sinners." No, it only says, "sinners." And I know this, that when I come, I come to Christ today . . . I dare not come as a conscious sinner or an awakened sinner, but I have to come still as a sinner with nothing in my hands.[9]

For your sake, Jesus lived a perfect life, he chose wisdom every time, and against intense seduction. Then Jesus died on the cross a death he did not deserve, a sacrificial death for the stupidity of the rest of us. That is what the gospel announces. If you will receive this Jesus by mere faith, he will give you his perfect record as a gift. He wants your conscience to be happy and free again. Why? Because *in the strength of being forgiven, you will change.* C. S. Lewis wrote to a friend, "You write much about your own sins. Beware . . . lest humility should pass over into anxiety or sadness. It is bidden us to 'rejoice and always rejoice.' Jesus has cancelled the handwriting which was against us. Lift up our hearts!"[10]

Knowing that Jesus covers your sin when you deserve to be exposed, but he accepts you and rejoices over you—that stunning new awareness will lift your heart and take you further with him than you have ever dreamed of going. His love creates your wise choice, moment by moment. Look up to him by faith, see his love for you right now, and receive it. Then, whatever might be your next step of obedience, that bold new step that maybe you have been putting off, you *will* take it. You will be able to choose, and you will choose wisely, to the praise of the glory of his grace.

15

The Tongue

PROVERBS 18:21

Death and life are in the power of the tongue.

18:21

"STICKS AND STONES MAY BREAK MY BONES, but words will never harm me." Not so. Words have power, far more than sticks and stones. Let's never think, if we speak recklessly, "It's only words. It's not like I'm *doing* anything." Words can penetrate to the heart. Derek Kidner writes, "What is done *to* you is of little account beside what is done *in* you . . . for good or ill."[1]

The fact that we speak at all is an obvious sign that God made us. God uses words. Animals do not. You might be able to teach a dolphin to say a few words, but you can't get a little child to shut up! Words mark us as human, in the image of God. Like God, we use words to create trust and form relationships and build community. But unlike God, we use words to destroy trust and break relationships and divide community. Like God, we use words for one heart to touch another heart at a deep level. But unlike God, we use words for one heart to break another heart at a deep level.

Our words matter—in conversations and emails and texts and blogs and phone calls and all the rest. Much of the strife in our families and offices and dorms and churches and nations is because of foolish words. But we often underestimate the importance of our words. Adultery, for example, is perceived in most Bible-believing churches as a serious sin. And it is. But I have never seen adultery send a whole church into meltdown. Gossip, by contrast, is often perceived as a little sin. But it destroys churches. Gossip

131

can even be perceived as some kind of need: "I *have* to let all this out!" As Americans, we do have the right of free speech. In our political culture we have the right—if it's a right, nobody can stop us—to blurt out whatever we feel. But when we become Christians, we enter a new culture where we surrender that right. We stop blurting out whatever we feel. We bring our words under the judgment of God's Word. The Bible says, "A fool gives full vent to his spirit, but a wise man quietly holds it back" (Proverbs 29:11). The Bible says of the power of the tongue, "How great a forest is set ablaze by such a small fire!" (James 3:5). Do you know how many people it takes to split a church? Not half the congregation. Just two. One to start spreading the fiery negativity, and another not to confront that behavior as the sin that it is.

The Bible gives us something better to talk about. The Bible simply changes the subject. Three times the risen Jesus greeted his disciples this way: "Peace be with you" (John 20:19, 21, 26). He set a new tone. If our tongues will come under the control of his peace, our churches will be safe places, sanctuaries for sinners. Then many people can meet Christ in our churches, and no one has the right to disturb that peace. It is sacred. It is blood-bought.

Chapters 1—9 of the book of Proverbs introduce the body of the book, chapters 10—31, where we read the actual proverbs themselves. But there is less literary arrangement in chapters 10—31. Chapters 1—9 consist of poems in praise of wisdom. But it often appears that the proverbs in chapters 10—31 "jump from one topic to another like scatterbrains in a living-room conversation."[2] Though there are subtle literary arrangements embedded in the body of the book, it is more helpful not to preach consecutively through these chapters. So at this point I will pull together various proverbs that cluster around topics.[3] The first topic is the power of words.

One of my commentaries on the book of Proverbs lists around ninety proverbs counseling us about how to speak.[4] In fact, the book of Proverbs has more to say about our words than anything else it addresses in our lives— more than money, sex, or family. One body of research reports that the average American speaks about 700 times per day.[5] If that number sounds high to you, cut it in half to 350 times per day. If it still sounds high, cut it in half again to 175 times a day. Still, there are very few things we do 175 times a day. Our many words matter. The Bible says, "Glorify God in your body" (1 Corinthians 6:20). Proverbs is saying, "That starts with your tongue."

Our Words: Moral Status

There is gold and abundance of costly stones,
but the lips of knowledge are a precious jewel. (Proverbs 20:15)

Our words are more than puffs of air coming up through our vocal cords. Our words have moral status in the sight of God. That "the lips of knowledge are a precious jewel" means that knowledgeable, informed, intelligent words are rare and valuable in God's eyes. We know what it is like to be listening to someone and it is obvious they do not know what they are talking about. We also know what it is like to fall silent whenever a certain person speaks, because whatever that person has to say is wise and helpful and almost a work of art. God is saying that high quality of speech is precious to him.

Lying lips are an abomination to the LORD. (Proverbs 12:22)

Lying might not bother us that much. Husbands and wives lie to each other. Advertisers lie. Politicians lie. It is just the way things have to be done sometimes—or so we are told. But that is deeply untrue. Maybe you have seen the film *Liar Liar* with Jim Carrey. An attorney comes under a spell, making him tell the truth for twenty-four hours. It is hilarious and embarrassing and ultimately redemptive. Well, hilarious, embarrassing, and redemptive is not a bad life. Better than abomination! Lying is *repulsive* to God. It may not make our skin crawl, but it really bothers God.

Jesus said the devil is "a liar and the father of lies" (John 8:44). Why is lying so evil? Because true, sincere, honest words bind us together in community. True words make love and trust and intimacy possible. But false words conceal us from one another, even as we might go on faking community, role-playing community outwardly while something else is really going on in our hearts. And who wants that hypocrisy? There is nothing divine in it.

But speaking lies is only half the problem. *Listening* to lies, gossip, flippant denigration—that is a moral issue too.

An evildoer listens to wicked lips,
   and a liar gives ear to a mischievous tongue. (Proverbs 17:4)

God wants us to know that just standing there and listening, tolerating the evil, shares in the evil. Listening is itself lying: "A *liar* gives ear to a mischievous tongue." We lie to ourselves that we are not involved because we are only listening. But listeners *are* involved. Be careful what you listen to. A person can become a "garbage collector." Someone in the group becomes the one to whom disgruntled people go, because that person will listen and sympathize and be a shoulder to cry on and a rallying point for complaints and a hero to those with hurt feelings. And that listener becomes a bigger problem in the group than the talkers.

But here is an alternative. If a person approaches you and starts criticizing someone else, you smile and interrupt and say, "Time out. I don't want to be involved in this. But the person you're talking about is right over there on the other side of the room. Let's you and I go right now and you tell that person to his face what you're telling me behind his back, okay?" If we will have the courage to obey God at that moment of temptation, our churches will be safe places where people never have to wonder what is really going on, and they can relax and enjoy themselves and grow in Christ. Our words have moral status at that level.

> The words of a whisperer are like delicious morsels;
>   they go down into the inner parts of the body. (Proverbs 18:8)

Let's all admit it. We *love* gossip. We *love* negative information about other people. We *love* controversy. We find it delicious. It is a delicacy—to our corrupt hearts. We gulp these words down with relish. But the contagion goes down into us and makes a deep impression and leaves us even sicker than we were before. Truly, God is not mocked.

> Open your mouth for the mute,
>   for the rights of all who are destitute.
> Open your mouth, judge righteously,
>   defend the rights of the poor and needy. (Proverbs 31:8, 9)

Do you speak up when others are put down? Or do you just stand there and listen in sinful silence as the blast of gossip and slander hits you in the face? God says, "Open your mouth." With every unkind word that goes unconfronted, a reputation dies.

So much is at stake in our words. They matter not just to us but even more, far more, to God. We are always speaking before the face of God.

Our Words: Emotional Power
Death and life are in the power of the tongue. (Proverbs 18:21)

The tongue can kill—literally. I heard about a woman in Los Angeles who took her own life. All she wrote in her suicide note was this: "They said." In his suicide note, Vince Foster of the Clinton White House wrote of Washington, "Here ruining people is considered sport." "Death [is] . . . in the power of the tongue." That is why Jesus said, "On the day of judgment people will give account for every careless word they speak" (Matthew 12:36). Words do not even have to be intentional to be deadly; they can be careless:

> There is one whose rash words are like sword thrusts,
> but the tongue of the wise brings healing. (Proverbs 12:18)

In English we speak similarly about "cutting remarks." It happens in an outburst of rash words, reckless words, unthinking words, just blurting out whatever we might be thinking without filtering it wisely. It is easy to do, but it is not easy for the other person to receive or to forget. We need to see in our rash words razor blades flying out of our mouths right into the body of the other person. Those wounds and scars remain long after the words have faded away. This is why there should never be shouting in a Christian home. If your teenager yells at you, here is what you say: "You don't have to like me. But you do have to respect me." And then you help your child to become respectful rather than rash. But if you do not teach your child to behave respectfully, then you are teaching your child to behave disrespectfully and to become a killer with his or her rash words. What you permit, you promote. And when your child, many years from now, splits a church by his or her sword-thrust words, God will hold you in part responsible.

But "life [is] . . . in the power of the tongue" too. "The tongue of the wise brings healing," the sage teaches us. Why? Because the tongue of the wise cares more about soothing an injury than winning an argument. Here are three simple but powerful words that bring healing: "I am sorry." Just those three little words: "I am sorry." In his prophetic book *The Mark of the Christian*, Francis Schaeffer taught us Christians how to love one another in healing ways:

> What does this love mean? How can it be made visible? First, it means a very simple thing. It means that when . . . I have failed to love my Christian brother, I go to him and say, "I'm sorry." . . . It may sound simplistic to start with saying we are sorry and asking forgiveness, but it is not. This is the way of renewed fellowship, whether it is between a husband and wife, a parent and child, within a Christian community, or between groups. When we have shown a lack of love toward the other, we are called by God to go and say, "I'm sorry. . . . I really am sorry." If I am not willing to say, "I'm sorry," when I have wronged somebody else—especially when I have not loved him—I have not even started to think about the meaning of a Christian oneness which the world can see. The world has a right to question whether I am a Christian. And more than that . . . if I am not willing to do this very simple thing, the world has a right to question whether Jesus was sent from God and whether Christianity is true.[6]

Time does *not* heal all wounds. Ignoring injuries does *not* make them go away. But wise words can and do bring healing. Going back and saying the humble, honest, beautiful things that need to be said is step one toward powerful healing.

But even when people do not have the tongue of the wise and do not say the things that would make such a positive difference, Jesus still does. Ultimately, the cruel things people say to us do not even matter. Ultimately, all that matters is the gospel things he says to us: "You are my beloved, in whom I am well-pleased." The Holy Spirit bears witness with your spirit that you are a child of God (Romans 8:16). And in a moment of crisis, when you might be too confused and hurt even to feel your place in his love, you are still his child. You *will* feel his love eventually, because the Holy Spirit has the lips of the wise, and he will bring healing as no one else can. That is the hopeful, cheering reality we want to spread to one another and to everyone who will listen to the gospel:

> Anxiety in a man's heart weighs him down,
>   but a good word makes him glad. (Proverbs 12:25)

We were not meant to stand alone! In our isolation we become depressed and fearful. Sometimes we are in two minds. We trust God, but we don't really trust God. So we need a good word from outside ourselves, a sta-bilizing word of hope from another Christian. The sage reminds us here that we can be speaking good words into each other's hearts. The message we speak, because it is the truth, might not be that the problem is going away; but the message can always be, "God is with you." I love the way Jonathan encouraged his despondent friend David and "strengthened his hand in God" (1 Samuel 23:16). It is good to be with one another in hard times. But what matters most is that *God* is always with us, for the sake of Christ. As that good and gladdening word spreads around among us, we are emboldened to do for Christ what we would never attempt alone. Dietrich Bonhoeffer wrote:

> The Christian needs another Christian who speaks God's Word to him. . . .
> The Christ in his own heart is weaker than the Christ in the word of his brother; his own heart is uncertain, his brother's is sure.[7]

One of the ways Jani and I pray while driving to church every Sunday morning is, "Lord, don't let one word come out of our mouths that isn't of you. Let every word we speak be of you." We want every word to be a bless-ing. Will you join us in praying that way as you drive to church? Good words make people glad in Christ. And when a whole church does that together, it starts feeling like revival.

The mouth of the righteous is a fountain of life. (Proverbs 10:11)

The lips of the righteous feed many. (Proverbs 10:21)

There is enough in Christ not only for us but also to refresh others. And it is our words that open his fountain and spread his table for many others. How do we get restocked ourselves? By going deeper with Christ. He is able, there in that place of deep communion with himself, to make our mouths into still waters and our lips into green pastures for others around us. The Bible says that our words, when we use them for Christ, "give grace to those who hear" (Ephesians 4:29). It isn't just the pastor who does that. God has called all of his people to this powerful privilege. In fact, when Proverbs 10:21 says "the lips of the righteous feed many," the word "feed" means "shepherd," the way a shepherd tends and guides and protects and feeds his flock of sheep. It means we all take responsibility to breathe life into everyone around us by our words of encouragement. That is how Jesus our Shepherd speaks through us.

But words alone can only do so much. That takes us to our next point.

Our Words: Practical Limitations

In all toil there is profit,
>   but mere talk tends only to poverty. (Proverbs 14:23)

"Mere talk" can be boastful or defeatist or just plain lazy. In a way, it is good always to be dreamers. Dreaming can be the first step toward a better future. But dreaming without working is no future, because words cannot substitute for deeds.

Here is another limitation. Words alone cannot change reality—and our excuses do not impress God:

If you say, "Behold, we did not know this,"
>   does not he who weighs the heart perceive it? (Proverbs 24:12)

God holds us responsible to be our brother's keeper. Who is suffering among the people you know, someone you can help, and what are you doing about it? Or are you just talking about it, or even looking the other way? When deeds are required, words are empty, and God is not fooled.

Here is another limitation. Your words cannot protect you, and they can expose you. In fact, they might give your enemies ammunition against you.

Whoever guards his mouth preserves his life;
>   he who opens wide his lips comes to ruin. (Proverbs 13:3)

Jesus was the only person in all of history who never spoke an unguarded, self-indulgent word. He never opened his lips in a wrong way, not once, ever. He never spoke when silence was better, and every word he did speak was perfect. Even his enemies said, "No one ever spoke like this man!" (John 7:46).

In a way, Jesus disproved Proverbs 13:3. His guarded mouth *didn't* preserve his life. His words were infallibly wise, and we felt outclassed, we felt threatened, we felt shamed, so we killed him—and he took it. Why? What happened at the cross? On the cross Jesus loved us so much that his sacrifice deleted the damning record before God of every foolish word you and I have ever spoken. He took the divine condemnation for our lies, insults, gossip, put-downs, bragging, false promises, and griping, as well as our guilty silence when we should have spoken up. He took it all onto himself and hit the delete button. Look at him on his cross, dying for what you and I have said and left unsaid. See him there, trust him, and you are finally free of it all forever.

As we consider these proverbs about our use of the tongue, every one of us is responding right now in either of two ways. Perhaps we are saying, "Thank you. Now I know what to do. And I can do this. These proverbs are so practical. They give me the wisdom I need. So here I go!" Or perhaps our response is, "Oh no, now I see how stupid I've been. I've alienated my wife. I've injured my kids. I've lost friends. I've been a fool, and I am so defeated. What's the point of even trying?" In other words, every one of us is either on the front end of foolish, disobedient words, and we do not see it coming, or we are on the back end of foolish, disobedient words, and we are suffering for it. But here is the gospel for all of us who are trusting in Christ: "You are accepted. You are not excluded. You are still in my conversation, because at the cross Jesus said, 'My God, my God, why are you not speaking to me?' God stopped communicating acceptance to his Son, so that he would never stop communicating acceptance to us. Will you believe that?"

If you are willing to be forgiven that way, you will also be humble enough to let Jesus be your speechwriter from now on. The Bible calls him the Word (John 1:1, 14), everything that needs to be said, the only thing that needs to be said.

The final point in this study is *how* his wisdom gets inside us.

God's Words: Our Life and Future

You have been born again, not of perishable seed but of imperishable, through the living and abiding word of God; for "All flesh is like grass and all its glory like the flower of grass. The grass withers, and the flower falls, but the word of the Lord remains forever." And this word is the good news that was preached to you. (1 Peter 1:23–25)

I was born mortal by the natural process, and it is only a matter of time until I die. I have also been reborn immortal by sheer miracle, and it will never end. How did that happen for me? How does it happen for anyone? Through the gospel, "the living and abiding word of God." And to this day, whenever I hear the good news of God's grace, I come alive all over again. That is how God renews all of us—through the gospel message of his love for sinners like me and you. The Spirit of God uses the Word of God to put new life in our hearts and new words in our mouths. What happened when the Holy Spirit came down at Pentecost? The risen Jesus filled the hearts of his people, and they could not stop praising him. It hasn't stopped since. It never will. Our words wither and fall. I think of the Top Ten hit songs from my senior year in high school. I love that music. It makes me happy. But does anyone else anymore? Who is going to care about our lyrics forty years from today? But God's Word remains; it will keep on giving new life, and it always will.

Just keep listening to the gospel, and God will keep renewing you all the way to Heaven. It will go deeper and deeper into you. And your words will spread new life to many other people too, with eternal impact.

16

Humility

PROVERBS 22:4

The reward for humility and fear of the LORD
is riches and honor and life.

22:4

PREACHING A SERMON (OR WRITING A CHAPTER) on humility is awkward. How can *I* preach such a sermon? Only by admitting up front that I am proud. But I would like to be humble, because Jesus is. You want to be humble too. So let's learn together from him. Everything he commands he also gives, and on terms of grace.

The theme of humility and openness and reasonableness and teachability is pervasive throughout the book of Proverbs. This book never stops begging us to keep learning. How can we grow in wisdom unless we are teachable? How can we change unless we are open to change? That upward growth trajectory requires humility. We walk into church saying to our Lord and Savior and Mentor, Jesus Christ, "We want newness of life, and we are coming to you for it. We are open to you. We are listening to you. Show us your glory. Take us further with you than we've ever gone before, further than we've ever dreamed of going." That radical openness is humility, and he promises to honor that humility.

The Bible is so clear. "Whoever exalts himself will be humbled, but whoever humbles himself will be exalted" (Matthew 23:12; Luke 14:11; 18:14). "God opposes the proud, but gives grace to the humble" (James 4:6; 1 Peter 5:5). "Whoever humbles himself like this child is the greatest in the kingdom of heaven" (Matthew 18:4). "Exalt that which is low, and bring low that which is exalted" (Ezekiel 21:26). "Every valley shall be lifted up, and every mountain and hill be made low" (Isaiah 40:4). This message is all over the Bible. It is basic to the ways of God. The irony is, pride humiliates us, and humility honors us.

We have at least an intuitive understanding of that. When we see a person who is full of himself and drawing attention to himself, what do we feel inside? Don't we want to cut him down to size, at least a little? And when we see someone else who is humble and lifting others up and doing a great job without expecting any thanks and so forth, don't we want to see him get some credit? He who exalts himself will be humbled, but he who humbles himself will be exalted—even for us, but far more with God. We walk into a better future not through self-exaltation but through humility before Christ. That is why C. J. Mahaney's book on humility says that pride is our greatest enemy and humility is our greatest friend.[1] God blesses the humble because, amazingly, God himself is humble.

What Is Humility?

The fear of the LORD is the beginning of knowledge;
    fools despise wisdom and instruction. (Proverbs 1:7)

The fear of the LORD is the beginning of wisdom,
    and knowledge of the Holy One is insight. (Proverbs 9:10)

The reward for humility and fear of the LORD
    is riches and honor and life. (Proverbs 22:4)

The fear of the Lord is not the spirit of our times. Self-esteem is the spirit of our times. I did a search on amazon.com for books on self-esteem, and I got 14,879 hits. The conventional wisdom of our times is that self-regard is how we become well-adjusted and successful; but if you lack self-esteem, you are on the road to underachieving and maybe even a life of crime. That is what we are told. But it isn't true. In her *New York Times* article "The Trouble with Self-Esteem," Lauren Slater quotes a researcher who studied criminals and concluded this: "The fact is, we've put antisocial men through every self-esteem test we have, and there's no evidence for the old psychodynamic concept that they secretly feel bad about themselves. These men are racist or violent because they don't feel bad enough about themselves."[2]

The Bible is not saying there is no place for a sense of personal worth. But that doesn't come first. The book of Proverbs takes us to another place for our starting point in wisdom. "*The fear of the LORD* is the beginning of wisdom." He comes first—not Self but Christ. He is our most urgent need and the key to our future. That is what the Bible is saying, and for us that is an adjustment. Bob Kauflin recently tweeted this: "My sin is that my heart is pleased or troubled as things please or trouble me, without my having a regard to Christ." A radical reorientation! When we start feeling the difference between self-esteem and Christ-esteem—that is when the idol of Self is losing its grip and Christ is saving us. It is the beginning of a whole new life.

But if we are humble at all, we have to wonder, "Am I humble *enough*? Do I fear the Lord *enough*? Look at my lust for being noticed, my self-pity, my melodramatic internal narrative, my grasping and clinging and calculating. If only I did fear the Lord!" But here is the good news. We do not come to Christ because we are humble. We come to Christ because we are proud, and he receives us and loves us and helps us in our pride. "The fear of the LORD is the beginning of wisdom," but the grace of the Lord is the beginning of the fear of the Lord. Jesus said in his parable of the wedding feast, "See, I have prepared my dinner . . . and everything is ready. Come to the wedding feast" (Matthew 22:4). He did not say *we* are ready; he said *the feast* is ready. So come. Don't worry if you are humble enough. You're not. Neither am I. But all of us can go to Christ right now, and moment by moment, because he promises everyone who comes to him riches and honor and life. Let your heart be melted by the grace of Christ. That is humility—all the humility you need to come into his feast.

Why Does Humility Matter?

> Blessed is the one who fears the LORD always,
>   but whoever hardens his heart will fall into calamity. (Proverbs 28:14)

The Hebrew word for "fears" in this proverb is different from the word in "The fear of the LORD is the beginning of wisdom." This word in 28:14 is more intense. It means to tremble, to shiver, to shake. And the B-line shows us that fearing the Lord is the opposite of a hard heart. It is the opposite of a flippant, blasé, unserious heart. But the irony here is the word "blessed," which is a happy word. It basically means "Congratulations!" The word "blessed" is a Biblical high-five. Do you see the surprise? The surprise is that meltdown before God is like a dam breaking with overflowing happiness. Emotional meltdown before God, when we see him as he really is and ourselves as we really are, sweeps away our internal barriers, the defensiveness that keeps God at a manageable distance and makes us so sad. But then the gospel breaks through and floods us in divine forgiveness. Getting past our image-management and trembling before God brings us deep happiness.

> The fear of the LORD is instruction in wisdom,
>> and humility comes before honor. (Proverbs 15:33)

> Before destruction a man's heart is haughty;
>> but humility comes before honor. (Proverbs 18:12)

> One's pride will bring him low,
>> but he who is lowly in spirit will obtain honor. (Proverbs 29:23)

These three proverbs summarize the message of the whole Bible: humility before honor, the cross before the crown. It is both the message of the Bible and the pattern of our own lives. First we take the courses and submit to the exams and all the rest, and then we graduate. It is just how life works, and it requires humility. Even God accepted it. The Apostle Peter read back through the entire Old Testament; then he looked at the life of Jesus, and he saw this pattern: suffering, then glory (1 Peter 1:10–12). That outlook became the template with which Peter saw everything in life. His entire first letter is embedded in this expectation: first humility, then honor.

We would rather skip the suffering and the humility and get right to the honor. So why accept the arrangement God has established? Because it works. It really is the only pathway to honor, and there is no other way. Our hearts long for what Peter calls "praise and glory and honor" (1 Peter 1:7), The Apostle Paul validates our desire for "glory and honor and immortality" (Romans 2:7). Everybody wants to write the next mega-hit. Everybody wants a place in the Hollywood Walk of Fame or the *Guinness Book of World Records* or whatever. Nobody wants to be a zero. For a person created in the image of God to be a zero is unbearable. And God himself *wants* to honor us. Here is the climax of his gospel: ". . . those whom he justified he also *glorified*" (Romans 8:30). That is not our proud overreaching. That is the grace of God. He is not out to make you mediocre; he is out to make you spectacularly glorious. But here is the surprising way he gets us there: "He who is lowly in spirit will obtain honor." This fraudulent world runs on swagger. And it doesn't look like that is ever going to change. But it will, because God has his own plans for this world and for you. Your life might not look like much right now. But don't worry about it. If you are trusting God for your significance, keep your eyes looking ahead at his promises. Even one of our own "prophets" has said,

The line it is drawn, the curse it is cast
The slow one now will later be fast
As the present now will later be past
The order is rapidly fadin'
And the first one now will later be last
For the times they are a-changin'[3]

Pride goes before destruction,
    and a haughty spirit before a fall. (Proverbs 16:18)

Whoever trusts in his own mind is a fool,
    but he who walks in wisdom will be delivered. (Proverbs 28:26)

There are those who are clean in their own eyes
    but are not washed of their filth. (Proverbs 30:12)

All the ways of a man are pure in his own eyes,
    but the LORD weighs the spirit. (Proverbs 16:2)

There is a way that seems right to a man,
    but its end is the way to death. (Proverbs 14:12)

The Hebrew words translated "pride" and "haughty" in Proverbs 16:18 both have to do with height, with being lifted up. The Bible says, in the book of Daniel, that the Most High God—that is his title, and it fits him—gave King Nebuchadnezzar glory and majesty. The Bible had no problem with that man holding world domination. But then it says, "When his heart was lifted up . . . so that he dealt proudly, he was brought down" (Daniel 5:20). The word translated "destruction" in Proverbs 16:18 means a breaking, like a bone being shattered. It is painful. It hurts when our egotistical dreams are broken and our proud self-images are shattered. But God is in it. So it's a healing blow. Here is a prayer God will never refuse: "Lord, keep me in your humility. Keep me down low before you, where I belong." Humility is the safest place for every one of us. I find it good for me sometimes, when I pray, to get down on my face. Not just on my knees—down on my face, as low as I can get. It is contrary to my pride, but that lowest place is where I belong before the Most High God. It is also the place of blessing.

We need to be deliberate about this, because we do not naturally see our pride: "All the ways of a man are pure in his own eyes." Pride feels normal. We trust in our own minds. We feel innocent. We feel more sinned against than sinning, like King Lear. But what matters is not how we feel but where we are going: "There is a way that seems right to a man, but its end is the way to death." The scariest thing about us is our glib self-assurance. We are not alarmed by ourselves. The on-ramps to the interstate of death have no warnings, no signs, no flashing red lights. But God is telling us. We need to pay attention.

I had lunch with a research psychiatrist at a major university. We were talking about the human brain. He said our brains are basically simple, even primitive. Our brains sense positives and tell us to move toward the positives. Our brains sense negatives and tell us to move away from the negatives. But as fallen beings, our wires get crossed. Our very brains lie to us. Our brains sincerely experience negatives as positives, and we want to move toward them. And our brains sincerely experience positives as negatives, and we want to move away from them. Another researcher arrives at this assessment:

> Your unscrupulous brain is entirely undeserving of your confidence. It has some shifty habits that leave the truth distorted and disguised. Your brain is vainglorious. It's emotional and immoral. It deludes you. It is pigheaded, secretive and weak-willed. Oh, and it's also a bigot. . . . Yes, thanks to the masquerading of an untrustworthy brain with a mind of its own, much of what you think you know is not quite as it seems.[4]

Paul called it "the flesh" (Romans 8:7), the very stuff we are made of. And how do we escape the pull of that? This is why we need to follow the Bible more than our own internal thought world. The Bible is a more reliable guide away from death and toward life than our own intuitions. The Bible warns us away from death that feels like life and toward life that sometimes feels like death. Which do you trust more—your hunches or the Bible? Humility before the Bible is a matter of life and death. That's why humility matters.

How Does Humility Behave?

Whoever despises the word brings destruction on himself,
    but he who reveres the commandment will be rewarded. (Proverbs 13:13)

The ear that listens to life-giving reproof
    will dwell among the wise. (Proverbs 15:31)

Whoever conceals his transgressions will not prosper,
    but he who confesses and forsakes them will obtain mercy. (Proverbs 28:13)

The three key words are "reveres," "listens," and "confesses." That is how humility behaves: it reveres, listens, and confesses, in that order. First, humility *reveres* the Word of God, but pride despises it. Wherever you turn in the Bible, remind yourself, "God has a blessing for me here." Never dismiss a single verse. Even if you don't understand it, you can still say, "I don't understand this yet, but I will not despise it. I will not dismiss it as irrelevant or archaic. This book is Jesus speaking to me, every word of it. I will swallow the Word whole, including the hard parts, out of reverence for him." He will reward that humility with more understanding, and you will grow.

Second, humility *listens* to life-giving reproof. We have no obligation to pay attention to abuse. But wise reproof is life-giving. What is reproof? It is correction. We don't like being corrected. But we *need* our feathers ruffled. It gives life. When was the last time you said to someone you trust, "Help me see myself. How can I improve?" If you are not in any relationship where you trust anyone enough to open up like that and then really listen, there is a reason. The reason is not that you cannot find someone good enough for you; the reason is your pride. But humbly listening to trusted correction is essential to entering into the community of the wise.

Third, humility *confesses* and *forsakes* sin. We would rather save face. But it is so freeing to confess our sins, especially to one another! When we confess and forsake our sins, we obtain mercy. The Hebrew word translated "mercy" is related to the word for a mother's womb. Why? Because God has a soft spot in his heart for sinners who open up and come clean. God envelops us in his tenderness and warmth when we confess and forsake our sins. Let's never confess one another's sins and create a shaming environment. Let's confess our own sins. Let's never think as a church, "Thank God we're not like those other churches" (see Luke 18:11). What arrogance! Let's confess our own sins. The most significant thing I have ever read, outside the Bible, comes from Jonathan Edwards's "Thoughts on the Revival":

> Spiritual pride tends to speak of other persons' sins with bitterness or with laughter and an air of contempt. But pure Christian humility rather tends either to be silent about these problems or to speak of them with grief and pity. Spiritual pride is very apt to suspect others, but a humble Christian is most guarded about himself. He is as suspicious of nothing in the world as he is of his own heart. The proud person is apt to find fault with other believers, that they are low in grace, and to be quick to note their deficiencies. But the humble Christian has so much to do at home and sees so much evil in his own heart and is so concerned about it that he is not apt to be very busy with other hearts. He is apt to esteem others better than himself.[5]

Do you know who ends up in Hell? Everyone who sincerely believes he deserves Heaven. Do you know who ends up in Heaven? Everyone who sincerely believes he deserves Hell but is saying to Jesus, "Be merciful to me, a sinner!"

Where Can We Find Humility?

> Though [Christ Jesus] was in the form of God, [he] did not count equality with God a thing to be grasped, but made himself nothing, taking the form of a servant, being born in the likeness of men. And being found in human form, he humbled himself by becoming obedient to the point of death, even death on a cross. Therefore God has highly exalted him and bestowed on him the name that is above every name, so that at the name of Jesus every knee should bow, in heaven and on earth and under the earth, and every tongue confess that Jesus Christ is Lord, to the glory of God the Father. (Philippians 2:6–11)

C. S. Lewis wrote that pride is "the complete anti-God state of mind."[6] Here we see why. Humility began in Heaven. We did not invent it. The Son of God revealed it. We lift ourselves up. The Son of God stepped down. Nothing is too good for us. Nothing was too low for the Son of God. We make ourselves big deals. The Son of God made himself nothing. We measure out our obedience one inch at a time, to keep control. The Son of God became obedient to the point of death, even death on a cross, for you and me.

And this humble God loves us proud sinners. He even wants to share his glory with us, and on terms of grace. The only price we pay is the loss of foolish ego. What a liberation!

What new step of self-humbling is God calling you to take as you follow his Son? Whatever it is, he will honor you as you take that next step. After humility, there is honor. After the cross comes a crown. God will keep to his own way. So enter in. Risk your everything on God's faithful promise. He will be true to you.

17

Family

Train up a child in the way he should go;
even when he is old he will not depart from it.

22:6

EVERYONE HAS A FAMILY. Young and old, married and single, male and fe-male—everyone is involved in some kind of family. So the book of Proverbs speaks to every one of us. How does God help us live wisely, even beauti-fully, in our family relationships? We all want that. God wants it. But we get there not primarily by sorting things out with one another but primarily by seeing Christ in a new way.

Husbands and Wives Growing in Wisdom Toward One Another

An excellent wife who can find?
  She is far more precious than jewels.
The heart of her husband trusts in her,
  and he will have no lack of gain. (Proverbs 31:10, 11)

The climax of the book of Proverbs is a poem in praise of the ideal woman (31:10–31). She is a role model. The phrase "an excellent wife" in 31:10 is, translated more literally, "a woman of strength." In fact, the Septuagint, the ancient Greek translation of the Hebrew Bible, reads "a manly woman." The ideal woman is *strong*. How so? This poem goes on to say that she works hard, she makes money, she is kind to the poor, she is fearless about the future, she enhances her husband's reputation, she speaks with wisdom—all this and more. Verse 17 sums it up: "She dresses herself with strength and makes her arms strong." And in her strength she is not competing with her husband. She is not going through an identity crisis over sexual politics. She is beyond that. She is giving herself away to her family and her community with wholehearted selflessness. She has high standards, and she sticks to them. A woman of this quality is rare: "An excellent wife who can find? She is far more precious than jewels."

Where the ESV says in verse 11, "[Her husband] will have no lack of gain," the word translated "gain" is "loot, plunder, the spoils of war." Why that wording? Because life is a struggle. This woman is not living in a perfect environment where life is a breeze. She is living in the real world, and she is up to the challenge. No wonder her husband trusts her. He feels honored to be her husband. This woman that God gave him is his greatest earthly treasure. In fact, there is only one person this husband trusts more than his wife, and that is Jesus Christ himself. She has won a deep place in his heart. She is "an excellent wife," and her husband cherishes her.

Right now some women might be feeling, "My standards have not been that high. I haven't gotten through to my husband at that level. I don't feel strong. I feel defeated." Here is what you need to know. When Abraham wanted a wife for his son, he sent off to a distant land to find her (Genesis 24). And when God wanted a wife for your husband, he reached across an infinite expanse from Heaven to earth to arrange the whole flow of history to bring you to your man. God sees you as the ideal woman for your husband—or your husband-to-be. God sees you as a precious gift, under Christ. God values you. And God's strong affirmation of you is where you get new strength to keep growing into more and more personal excellence.

Some of us men might be feeling, "I haven't trusted and valued and affirmed my wife as she deserves." Let's think about that, because the primary message here in the book of Proverbs is for us husbands and husbands-to-be, which is nearly all of us men. What does the word "husband" mean? We have the related English word "husbandry," that is, cultivation. And when the word "husband" is used as a verb, it means to cultivate. If you are a husband, here is your job: to cultivate and nurture your wife. Your lifetime impact on your wife should be that her life opens up more and more, and she is enabled to become all that God wants her to be. God is calling you, as her husband, so to care for her that in her latter years she will be thinking, "What a great life I've had! My husband understood me. He cared for me. He inspired me to grow in Christ."

How does a husband do that? Not by browbeating his wife—God doesn't treat us that way—but by encouraging her. It's here in Proverbs 31:

> Her children rise up and call her blessed;
>   her husband also, and he praises her:
> "Many women have done excellently,
>   but you surpass them all."
> Charm is deceitful, and beauty is vain,
>   but a woman who fears the LORD is to be praised.
> Give her the fruit of her hands,
>   and let her works praise her in the gates. (vv. 28–31)

Her children rise up, they stand up, and they speak respectfully to their mom. They tell her why they esteem her, why they admire her as a woman of God. Where did the kids learn that? From dad: ". . . he praises her" (Proverbs 31:28). The key word in these verses is "praise." It appears three times in these verses. A husband cultivates his wife by setting a high tone of praise in their home. No putdowns. No fault-finding. No insults. Not even neutral silence. But rather bright, positive, life-giving *praise*. The picture here is of the wise woman giving herself to her family and to others, and she is receiving praise from her husband and children at home and from her community "in the gates." God wants to fill our homes and our churches with this beautiful wisdom, where men are not passive but overtly cultivating the excellence of their wives, and those women are thriving.

What is it that the wise husband says? "Many women have done excellently, but you surpass them all." How does *your* wife excel? Tell her. Tell her in front of the children. Have this conversation at the dinner table tonight—and tomorrow night. And if you cannot think of any way in which your wife excels and truly deserves to be praised, then that is your fault, because God called you to husband her into excellence. Is your wife becoming magnificent because she married you? The word "excellently" in verse 29 is the same word translated "excellent" in verse 10. God wants to see your wife become more and more capable because of your influence in her life. And he wants to hear you and your kids cheering her on all the way.

Men, this is not a pep talk. This is the gospel. This is about God. How you see God will inevitably show up in how you treat your family. You can fake it at work, but you cannot fake it at home. How you *really* see God—not what you're supposed to believe about God but what you really believe—will show up in how you treat your wife. A. W. Tozer wrote, "The essence of idolatry is the entertainment of thoughts about God that are unworthy of him."[1] If your concept of God is beneath who he really is, then you will have unworthy thoughts about your wife and unworthy words to her. And the problem is not her. The root problem is, your Jesus is not the real Jesus. Your Jesus is not big enough to set you free. If you cannot bring yourself to praise your wife and you live with her in silent, sullen, defeated mediocrity, there is a reason. The reason is how you see Christ. It may be that you have no complaints about him. He may seem to you an unobjectionable Savior. But if you have no passion for him, it's because you do not see in him mighty passion for you and a mighty salvation for you and a glorious future for you. That vision of Christ is unworthy of him. The truth is, the Lord Jesus Christ is a glorious Savior. Believe it. See him in his grace and glory toward you, rejoicing over you with all his mighty heart. It will change how you treat your wife—and a lot more.

My dad grew up in a Swedish-American home where they did not express love as freely as he desired. They were good people, but it just wasn't their way to open up about the deep things of the heart. But it is God's way. Dad understood that about God. So when Dad got married and started his own home, he made a decision. He decided to launch a new tradition. And I grew up in a home where we openly expressed our love for each other. It did not take three or four generations for this newness of life to evolve. Dad changed it suddenly because of who God is. Some of my best memories are the family sitting around the dinner table and Dad saying, "Let's take time now to affirm each other." He set that loving tone. It was the gospel at work in our home. That is what God can do for your family too, starting today.

Men, let's repent of our silence and the sin of withheld love. Have we robbed our families of the love they deserve? Have we truly and worthily represented Christ to our families? Or have we in effect denied the gospel in our homes? And here is a basic principle for us men: If we don't get radical, nothing will ever change. Christ got radical for you at the cross, and it changed everything forever. And he put you with your wife because he loves her. He put you with her as a mighty blessing to her. So get radical, start changing, begin a new tradition in your home, starting today. If you step out in new obedience, the Lord will help you. And your family will rejoice over you.

Children Growing in Wisdom Toward Their Parents

> A wise son makes a glad father,
>> but a foolish man despises his mother. (Proverbs 15:20)

> If one curses his father or his mother,
>> his lamp will be put out in utter darkness. (Proverbs 20:20)

Let your father and mother be glad;
    let her who bore you rejoice. (Proverbs 23:25)

Every one of us has a dad and a mom. So God is speaking to all of us here. How can we grow in wisdom toward our parents? The key words in Proverbs 15:20 and 20:20 are "despises" and "curses." Those words are the opposite of wisdom. What is the way of wisdom? The fifth commandment: "Honor your father and your mother" (Exodus 20:12). And that command not to despise, not to curse, but to honor our parents—that command applies to us all our life long, even after we grow up and leave home.

What is God saying? To "despise" our parents is to treat them as worthless. To "curse" our parents does not mean to swear at them but, like "despise," to treat them as beneath us. And to "honor" our parents is to treat them as weighty and worthy, just because they are our parents. They do not have to earn our respect; we owe it to them. The burden is not on them but on us—according to the Word of God. That helps teenagers who sometimes think their parents are dumb. God says, even if you do think your parents are dumb, you still owe them respect.

How can all of us fulfill our obligation to honor our parents? We do not have to agree with them. We do not even have to stay close to them. Sometimes a little distance helps. But we can honor them in two ways. First, we can thank them. We can stop blaming them for their failures and thank them for their successes. Even if your parents were not Christians, if they taught you right from wrong with the understanding they had, they did their job. Thank them. Let them know they made an impact that you appreciate now. Second, if your parents were Christians, imitate them. The Bible says, "Remember your leaders, those who spoke to you the word of God . . . and imitate their faith" (Hebrews 13:7). It does not say, "Imitate their style." The style is passé. The faith endures—or at least it deserves to. My own parents lived out the Christian faith. In our home, Jesus Christ was loved, and the Bible was revered, and we were expected to live as Christians. The cause of Christ was the defining center of our home. If we ran short of money, we still tithed because Christ comes first. That is the faith. And God is saying, "Don't let that faith die. Keep it burning for a new generation." We can honor our Christian parents by reproducing in our wishy-washy times an all-out Christian faith. And our parents will rejoice over us, even as the styles change.

Parents Growing in Wisdom Toward Their Children

Train up a child in the way he should go;
    even when he is old he will not depart from it. (Proverbs 22:6)

Your few years with your kids are a life-shaping opportunity. It might feel, right now, as though these high-commitment, child-rearing years will never end. But they will, and soon. Right now is your moment for enduring impact. There is more at stake for your child than getting into the best schools and the best sports and the best jobs. Your child has an eternal destiny. God has called you to train up your child to go to Heaven. That is ultimately "the way he should go." How do you help your child get there?

The word translated "train up" means "dedicate." Dedicate your child to Christ. Do not raise your child for the American Dream. Warn your child against the American Dream. It is an easy way to Hell. Your parental role is to raise your child to be gung-ho for Christ. The Hebrew word translated "train up" is related to an Arabic verb that was used of rubbing the palate of a newborn child with a date mixture, to get the child to suck. It means to accustom a child to a taste and to motivate the child to take it in. And the best way for you to influence your child in that way is for you to be a dedicated Christian yourself. Children sense hypocrisy immediately. But they also know sincerity. If you want your children to be passionate for Christ, let them see that passion in you. You dedicate your child to Christ by dedicating yourself to Christ so enthusiastically that your child tastes how good it is and wants more. Francis Schaeffer wrote:

> One of the greatest injustices we do to our young people is to ask them to be conservative. Christianity today is not conservative, but revolutionary. To be conservative today is to miss the whole point, for conservatism means standing in the flow of the status quo. . . . [W]e must teach the young to be revolutionaries, revolutionaries against the status quo.[2]

As our children enter young adulthood especially, they learn to love that revolutionary spirit and passion and boldness. What a joy it is, as a parent, to be the one to give it to them, for the sake of Jesus Christ!

> Folly is bound up in the heart of a child,
> but the rod of discipline drives it far from him. (Proverbs 22:15)

But there is another dynamic at work in our kids. Let's be realistic about it. This word "folly" means "the willful refusal to make moral choices."[3] This folly is your child's natural heart that does not want to grow up and enter adulthood with its moral demands. That folly is deep inside a child's heart. But in our world today we no longer object to it. It used to be that boys became men by age twenty-one. But today we have a new category between boyhood and manhood, a prolonged adolescence. "More people in their 20s are living with their parents. About one-fourth of 25-year-old white men lived at home in 2007—before the last recession—compared with one-fifth in 2000 and less than one-eighth in 1970."[4] These are men who are still boys. They don't know what they want, they don't make money, they don't get married, they don't have kids, they don't buy a house, they don't know what they believe, they don't contribute to the community. But God calls boys into adulthood, even before they feel ready:

- Joshua was Moses' assistant from his youth (Numbers 11:28).
- God called Samuel into the ministry when he was a boy (1 Samuel 3).
- David was anointed king as a young man (1 Samuel 16).
- Josiah, the reformer king, was eight years old when he began to rule (2 Kings 22, 23).
- Daniel was a young man when he stood up to Babylonian culture (Daniel 1).
- Timothy was young enough to be called "my child" by Paul but was entrusted with the responsibility to lead the church into the post-apostolic era (1 Timothy 4:12; 2 Timothy 2:1).
- John Quincy Adams was appointed by Congress as diplomatic secretary to the Court of Catherine the Great of Russia when he was fourteen years old. A year later he traveled unaccompanied for six months from St. Petersburg to Paris, stopping along the way in Stockholm to negotiate trade between the U.S. and Sweden.
- David Farragut went to sea at age ten, fought in the War of 1812 at age eleven, and by age twelve rose to the rank of captain and commanded a captured British ship.
- Charles Haddon Spurgeon preached his first sermon at age fifteen, pastored a church at sixteen, and at nineteen was preaching to crowds of 5,000 people in London.[5]

Our children have immaturity in their hearts, but they also have greatness in Christ. We parents help them out of the immaturity and into the greatness with the rod of discipline. It is hard to read the Bible and get the impression that children should never be spanked. You have to figure out how it works best in your home, and some kids need only a stare to melt their hearts. But every child needs coaching and punishments and rewards that help them grow up and become men and women of destiny.

In the fear of the LORD one has strong confidence,
    and his children will have a refuge. (Proverbs 14:26)

The greatest legacy we can leave our kids is how to find refuge in God when everything is on the line. Inevitably life gets harder than we ever dreamed it would be. At those moments of intense anguish, when godly parents bow down and trust Christ, they are teaching their children by a powerful example. They are teaching their children how to draw strength from God in suffering. And those kids in their day will also find a refuge in God when they suffer, as inevitably they will. I remember a man in my boyhood church who was dying of cancer and suffering intensely. My dad went to see him in the hospital and asked him gently and plainly, "Rolf, would you like to die?" And Rolf said, "No, Ray. This might be the greatest day of my life." Whatever else that man left to his family, that is a great legacy of faith!

All of Us Growing in Wisdom from the Lord

> Have you forgotten the exhortation that addresses you as sons? "My son, do not regard lightly the discipline of the Lord, nor be weary when reproved by him. For the Lord disciplines the one he loves, and chastises every son whom he receives." It is for discipline that you have to endure. God is treating you as sons. (Hebrews 12:5–7)

Everything depends on how we see God. When we suffer, it is easy to see God as harsh and demanding and brutal. Suffering feels like rejection. It feels like abandonment. It feels like loss. But the truth is, God is treating us as sons. God is leading us into maturity and wisdom and greatness. Some things in our lives we urgently need to lose. They are like Gollum's ring, way too precious to us. But losing our false prizes and gaining Christ, we enter into One who is worthy to be prized and will never be taken from us. Christ himself suffered. He was a perfect son of God, and even he learned the hard way (Hebrews 5:8). Can that be unacceptable to you and me?

But Jesus also suffered in a way we never will. At the cross he really was rejected, so that we will never be rejected. He really was abandoned, so that we will always be held close. He was utterly lost, so that we would be wonderfully found. He was treated as an outcast and even an enemy, so that we would be treated as family forever. Whatever else God is doing in your life today, however painful it may be, if you are in Christ, God is not forsaking you, God is not dismissing you, God is not hostile toward you. He is treating you as a son, a beloved son in whom he is well pleased, for the sake of Christ his Son. His fatherly heart is drawing you in and taking you deeper because he treasures you and rejoices over you and understands you and has a magnificent future for you.

Will you trust him and take your next step forward?

18

Emotions

PROVERBS 15:30

*The light of the eyes rejoices the heart,
and good news refreshes the bones.*

15:30

IN THE BOOK OF PROVERBS, God our Father is coaching us in strategies for newness of life. What does gospel newness look like specifically and practically, including our emotions? And why *not* emotions? God is emotional. Look at Jesus. He was God among us, and he was emotional.[1] He had to be emotional. Emotion is part of humility. Jesus did not stand aloof but got involved. One of the ideals of the Stoics was απαθεια, freedom from the turbulence of emotion, living above all that. Jesus would have failed as a Stoic. The Bible says, "Surely he has borne our griefs and carried our sorrows" (Isaiah 53:4). He entered in wholeheartedly, to redeem our fallen emotions.

How do we see real and perfect emotion in Christ? In many ways. But his primary feeling in this world was compassion. He looked at the rich young man and "loved him" (Mark 10:21). He was "moved with pity" by the leper (Mark 1:41). He "wept" over Lazarus (John 11:35). He wailed over Jerusalem (Luke 19:41). He "sighed" over the deaf man (Mark 7:34). Jesus cared deeply, and he still does today. Wherever the gospel goes, people's compassion is aroused. Paul wrote, "I yearn for you all *with the affection of Christ Jesus*" (Philippians 1:8). The heart of Christ melted this stuck-up Pharisee's heart with yearning and affection. And today the emotions of the risen Christ are flowing into the world through us as we humble ourselves

157

and get involved. Gospel emotions are a vital part of the display of Christ to the world today. Emotions are a major way we create a gospel culture in our churches, where people can experience a compassion that comes from God.

But Jesus felt more than tenderness and compassion. He also got angry. He was angry at the Pharisees. He "looked around at them with anger, grieved at their hardness of heart" (Mark 3:5). When his own disciples wanted to shoo the children away, he was irritated, and he showed it (Mark 10:14). He was angrily offended at death when he stood at the grave of a friend (John 11:33, 38). He busted up the moneychangers in the temple (John 2:13–17), and the Bible says he made the whip himself (v. 15). So it wasn't a mere outburst. He really meant it. He also called people "pigs" (Matthew 7:6). He called people "hypocrites" (Matthew 15:7). He called people "wolves" (Matthew 7:15). Jesus never wavered in openly resenting what's wrong with our world.

But he went beyond anger at wrong. He also suffered for it. The Bible calls him "a man of sorrows" (Isaiah 53:3). He took our sorrows as his own. He did not have to, but emotional vulnerability is part of the price love is willing to pay. His heart was tormented in his Passion. He said, "Now is my soul troubled" (John 12:27), and "My soul is very sorrowful, even to death" (Matthew 26:37, 38). On the cross he felt the flames of Hell, he smelled the smoke of Hell. But he endured the cross for a reason, and that reason was "the joy that was set before him" (Hebrews 12:2). The Bible says that Jesus was anointed with "the oil of gladness beyond his companions" (Psalm 45:7). In other words, he was the happiest man of all. The Bible says that "he rejoiced in the Holy Spirit" (Luke 10:21). That is high-octane joy. He told us why he came: ". . . that my joy may be in you, and that your joy may be full" (John 15:11). He did not come to give us an emotionless ethic; he came to give us the fullness of his joy. He did not come into this world with a burning sense of wrong but with a happy sense of mission. And he lived in close fellowship with God all the way.[2] How could Jesus not be a happy man? I want you to see Jesus Christ in all the fullness of his personal magnitude and beauty. It's who he is today, right now.

Jesus lived for us, in our place, the perfect human life, with every emotion in close alignment with the heart of God. And here in the book of Proverbs we have his wisdom for *our* emotions—our squally emotions, our negative emotions, our dead emotions, our distorted emotions, our upset emotions, our excessive emotions. We need the emotional life of Christ, and he wants to give it to us.

Our basic flaw is what the New Testament calls "desire." For example, "Each person is tempted when he is lured and enticed by his own desire.

Then desire when it has conceived gives birth to sin, and sin when it is fully grown brings forth death" (James 1:14, 15). The word there for "desire" means something like "emotion in overdrive." It is the death-creating power inside us. It shows up in our wacko emotions. Let's never think that just because we feel something honestly and effortlessly and sincerely, therefore it's an okay feeling. We sinners sin honestly and naturally. We do not have to try. It surges out of us from deep within. But the gospel remedy is not zero emotion. Christ finds us and receives us as emotional jungles, but he does not turn us into emotional deserts. He cultivates us as emotional gardens, with life and color and order, where our drivenness and compulsiveness and all the rest are redeemed into a holy and beautiful freedom and intensity. That is gospel emotion, given by grace. If you are out of control, or just dead inside, give yourself to Christ today. His heart is open to you right now. Let's open ourselves now to his wisdom.

Fear and Boldness

> The fear of the LORD is the beginning of knowledge;
>   fools despise wisdom and instruction. (Proverbs 1:7)

> The fear of the LORD is the beginning of wisdom,
>   and the knowledge of the Holy One is insight. (Proverbs 9:10)

> The wicked flee when no one pursues,
>   but the righteous are bold as a lion. (Proverbs 28:1)

One of the reasons we don't fear the Lord enough is that we fear people too much. We fear their disapproval. We get our okayness from the approval we sense from other people. But wisdom redirects our hunger for approval. Whose smile will really satisfy us? If God approves us up front, on terms of grace, that satisfies. If you are in Christ today, God wants you to know that your relationship with God tomorrow is pre-approved. God will correct you as needed, but he will not reject you, because Christ has already won God's approval for you. That assurance continually draws our hearts on toward him. The Bible says that when we are filled with spiritual wisdom, our goal changes; we want to be "fully pleasing to him" (Colossians 1:9, 10). We'd *like* to please everybody. But we *must* please him. That is the fear of the Lord. Wouldn't it be great to stop fearing people so much?

Here is how. If the fear of the Lord is the beginning of wisdom, the fear of man is the beginning of folly. Let's all admit, that is a real problem among us. We are always performing, hoping for applause. Then we can consider ourselves successful; then we can feel good about our lives. We even perform in front of ourselves, in the theater of our minds. We are constantly going onstage to build emotional capital from human applause and attention. But it's all false. What if people find out what frauds we really are? Here's our manmade religion. Our god is human approval. Our heaven is the spotlight. Our hell is bad reviews. Our ritual of worship is keeping up appearances. We have the wrong fear. And that wrong fear is the beginning, the entry point, the thin edge of the wedge for folly. Living a lie hollows us out. We end up so insecure, we flee when no one is even pursuing us—always fugitives, never settled and at peace.

To fear the Lord means his opinion is the only one that finally matters to our hearts. And he *promises* his approval through Christ. The gospel puts Christ onstage and says to us, "His performance is your review. You can stop posing. You can stop fearing exposure. You can stop looking back over your shoulder and worrying about the sins of yesterday. You can know for certain today that goodness and mercy will follow you all the days of your life, because of Christ." If you fear the Lord enough to let that gospel satisfy you, you will be bold and confident and valiant as a lion, like Christ himself.

Anger and Restraint

Hatred stirs up strife,
but love covers all offenses. (Proverbs 10:12)

Good sense makes one slow to anger,
and it is his glory to overlook an offense. (Proverbs 19.11)

A man of wrath stirs up strife,
and one given to anger causes much transgression. (Proverbs 29:22)

Whoever is slow to anger has great understanding,
but he who has a hasty temper exalts folly. (Proverbs 14:29)

Whoever is slow to anger is better than the mighty,
and he who rules his spirit than he who takes a city. (Proverbs 16:32)

We all feel anger. And not all anger is wrong. In fact, the closer we get to Christ, the angrier we will get at real evil. By nature we are cowards and compromisers. We need holy anger if we are going to represent the real Jesus to our world today. But it is so hard to sort out which anger is good and which anger is bad, isn't it? The book of Proverbs helps us get to the point. What do we *do* with our anger?

The anger that is hatred "stirs up strife." The word translated "strife" in

Proverbs 10:12 has to do with judgments, opinions. It's when someone walks up and demands of you, "So what do *you* think about _____?"—as if you are *expected* to have a strong opinion. But wisdom is not intimidated by that approach. Wisdom asks, "*Why* should I feel intensely about that issue? Moreover, why does anybody *need* my opinion? Why are we even talking about this? Is this issue the gospel?" Twitter and blogs and emails would be cleared of much conflict if we humbled our opinions before Christ. What are we here for, really? What does *God* want to be stirred up in our hearts? He says, stir one another up to love and good deeds (Hebrews 10:24).

Even if you are angry for good reason—sometimes there is real provocation—still, it is a *glory* to overlook a personal offense (Proverbs 19:11). We have a higher standard than getting even. Our standard is glory, because God is glorious. He overlooks our offenses because of the cross. He does not embarrass us. He is above that. God is beautiful. There is more than one word in the Old Testament for "glory," and this word in Proverbs 19:11 means "beauty." This word is used to describe beautiful clothing (Isaiah 52:1), beautiful jewels (Ezekiel 16:17), a beautiful city (Isaiah 28:1), and the beauty of God himself (1 Chronicles 29:11). He makes beautiful people who know how to ignore a slight. They judge themselves instead.

Anger is a judging emotion. Anger is our hearts feeling that something is wrong. And a lot *is* wrong. But wisdom brings this judging emotion itself under judgment. Fools unleash it without filtering it. In so doing, they exalt, they lift up for everyone to see, their own folly (Proverbs 14:29). But the wise rule their emotions with a nobility that outclasses world conquerors: "He who rules his spirit is better than he who takes a city" (Proverbs 16:32). Conquering a city is child's play compared with ruling the turbulent, demanding, upset world inside us. The one is only the battle of a day. The other is the conflict of a lifetime.[3]

Here is how the gospel helps us rule our anger moment by moment—the doctrine of the wrath of God. Christ is coming again in wrath to punish all evil with terrible finality. That is the clear teaching of the Bible. It is a great resource for tolerance and patience right now. Miroslav Volf put it well: "The certainty of God's just judgment at the end of history is the presupposition for the renunciation of violence in the middle of it."[4] If you really believe Christ will come in final and inescapable judgment, you don't need to be anyone's judge right now. The Lord Jesus Christ has all the wrath this world needs.

Jealousy and Tranquillity

> Wrath is cruel, anger is overwhelming,
>   but who can stand before jealousy? (Proverbs 27:4)

Anger can be violent, but jealousy is worse. Here's why. Anger at its best is reacting against something that is wrong. But jealousy is reacting against something that is right and good. If you wrong someone, they might forgive you. But if you're better than someone, they might never forgive you. Jealousy is that bad. Cain did not kill Abel because Abel had wronged him. "Why did he murder him? Because his own deeds were evil and his brother's righteous. Do not be surprised, brothers, that the world hates you" (1 John 3:12, 13). The Bible says it was out of envy that the enemies of Christ brought him down (Matthew 27:18). And the early church was persecuted because of jealousy (Acts 5:17, 18; 13:45). Who can stand before jealousy? It will keep coming after you relentlessly, until you come down to its level. If you refuse to knuckle under, it will punish you—and blame you for it all. This is one of the reasons we admire the Apostle Paul. When he was put in prison and had to cancel all his preaching gigs, other preachers in the early church were glad. With Paul out of the way, they finally got the limelight. Was Paul jealous and resentful? He was happy, because Christ was being preached, even out of bad motives (Philippians 1:12–18). When Christ, not Self, is who matters most to us, that frees us to be happy even when we are shoved aside, overlooked, passed by.

> A tranquil heart gives life to the flesh,
>   but envy makes the bones rot. (Proverbs 14:30)

Joseph Epstein's book on envy says that of the seven deadly sins, only envy is no fun at all.[5] It decays not only the soul but also the body: "Envy makes the bones rot." So how can you tell if envy is rotting you away? Ask yourself this: That person you resent—does it irritate you when he succeeds, and would it make you happy to see him fall? When you look at that person, is all you can see what is wrong with him and never what is right about him? Of course, you and I are complex individuals! *We* cannot be understood without taking a lot of nuances into account. But everyone we envy is easily categorized and dismissed! Obviously that is not the mind of Christ, nor the spirit of the gospel, nor the wisdom of Solomon. It is selfishness. And it's no fun.

But let's say the person you dislike really is horrible. Really. Some people are. Here is the wisdom of Christ for you:

Fret not yourself because of evildoers,
    and be not envious of the wicked,
for the evil man has no future;
    the lamp of the wicked will be put out. (Proverbs 24:19, 20)

If anyone is truly evil and successful—we don't envy losers—that brightly shining, impressive, formidable, evil person will be snuffed out and will come to nothing under the judgment of Christ. Can you think of one evil person in all of history who ended up with a life you want for yourself? Can you name even *one*? Why then do we fret? Why do we burn up inside with envy? Do we believe in Christ—really? Is his story big enough in our minds? The Lord of the Rings would not be the epic it is without Gollum. To quote Gandalf, "My heart tells me that he has some part to play yet, for good or ill, before the end."[6] Don't you think God is wise enough to manage that in real life?

Cheerfulness and the Gospel

All the days of the afflicted are evil,
    but the cheerful of heart has a continual feast. (Proverbs 15:15)

A joyful heart is good medicine,
    but a crushed spirit dries up the bones. (Proverbs 17:22)

The light of the eyes rejoices the heart,
    and good news refreshes the bones. (Proverbs 15:30)

We have been lied to about how to be happy. We have been told that we will finally be happy when we get our perfect little world assembled around us just the way we like it. It feels true, even obviously true. But it isn't. External things *cannot* satisfy an internal longing. Which is perfect, really. It means that when life is hard, even then a real cheerfulness can still treat us to a feast deep within. That feast is the love of God for us in Christ.

Here is how God gives that deep happiness. He sends someone to you, someone whose heart he has touched. You can see it in his or her eyes: "The light of the eyes [of one person] rejoices the heart [of another person]." The gospel makes people "radiant" (Psalm 34:5). So, a gospel-radiant person comes to you to say, in effect, "God isn't what you think. You think he hates you. You think his primary emotion toward you is disgust. But you're projecting onto him your own feeling. You hate him. That's what's happening here. You feel that way because you have sinned against him, but you're too proud to admit it's all your own fault. So you make it his fault. You think he's out to ruin you. And you think that's why your life is hard. But God isn't against you. He isn't out to accuse you. God himself has already answered every accusation against you at the cross of Christ—if you'll receive it. We are more loved than we ever dreamed. If you will open up and trust Christ, the accusations are over forever. God's power is greatest not in destroying sinners but in taking their sin onto himself at the cross and freely, happily giving back love. He loves *you* in that way. He loves you in the way your heart longs to be loved—not with a shallow pep talk or cheap flattery but with real forgiveness and acceptance and joy." God sends someone to tell you that, so that you can know it and let it in. The joy of the gospel is contagious. The light of the gospel rejoices the open heart.

You can feel alive again by pressing that gospel into your heart. Will you? God is ready to receive you right now.

19

Friendship

PROVERBS 18:24

There is a friend who sticks closer than a brother.

18:24

WISDOM IS WHEN WE OUTGROW our misconceptions about how life should work, and we learn how God actually built life to work, and work well. That takes us way beyond petty rule-keeping. Something deeper happens. God's wisdom enters our hearts and changes us within, so that as we grow, we know intuitively what to do and what not to do, what will work and what won't. Wisdom is skill for living when there is no obvious rule to go by. That is what the book of Proverbs is for—gospel wisdom for complicated lives.

A major area where wisdom helps us is friendship. So much is at stake in our friendships. And so much of friendship is a matter of feel. God has wisdom for us today about the nuances of real friendship. But it all begins with God himself.

God is our Friend through Christ. In fact, friendship began within God. It's who God is—Father, Son, and Spirit in eternal, powerful interactions of love. The heart of God is friendship reaching out.

We get an insight into our own hearts from the Assyrian king Adad-Nirari II (911–891 B.C.). He looked at himself and said: "*I am* royal, *I am* lordly, *I am* mighty, *I am* honored, *I am* exalted, *I am* glorified, *I am* powerful, *I am* all-powerful, *I am* brilliant, *I am* lion-brave, *I am* manly, *I am* supreme, *I am* noble."[1] My guess is, he did not have many friends. Self-important people don't. Now, God also made much of "I am" (Exodus 3:14). But what did the real "I Am" do with all his mighty being? In that passage God said, "I will be *with you*" (Exodus 3:12). That is a friend. A friend is there for *you*.

Jesus said, "No longer do I call you servants, for the servant does not know what his master is doing; but I have called you friends, for all that I have heard from my Father I have made known to you" (John 15:15). Back in the Old Testament, it was an honor to be called "the servant of the Lord." That privilege did not belong to just anybody. The prophets, for example, were the Lord's servants (Jeremiah 35:15). But it is an even higher honor to be the Lord's friend. The Bible says, "The LORD used to speak to Moses face to face, as a man speaks to his friend" (Exodus 33:11). Nobody else could get that close. But now, because of Christ, you and I have been drawn in. In that spirit, the Apostle John sent greetings from one church to another this way: "Peace be to you. The friends greet you. Greet the friends, every one of them" (3 John 15). God is befriending us, including us, drawing more and more people in. Friendship began in Heaven, not on earth, and is coming down to earth through the gospel today. The wisdom of Proverbs guides us into the strong friendships God is creating. God is saying to you right now, "Let's be friends. And let's win more friends—wisely."

What Is a Friend?

Many a man proclaims his own steadfast love,
but a faithful man who can find? (Proverbs 20:6)

A friend loves at all times,
and a brother is born for adversity. (Proverbs 17:17)

A faithful friend who loves at all times—that person is *rare*. "A faithful man *who can find?*" A brother is stuck with you. A brother is obligated to be some kind of safety net. That is what family is for. But a friend chooses you. When someone loves you at all times, good and bad, and they don't have to but they choose to—that person is a friend. A true friend is rock-solid. How many people like that do you know, compared with those who smile and make promises and create expectations but do not follow through? Human nature without the power of God is shallow *and self-congratulatory*: "Many a man proclaims his own steadfast love." But when you find a true friend, prize him. The gospel creates those rare people. The Bible says that the people of God "keep their promises even when it hurts" (Psalm 15:4, NLT) and "show themselves to be entirely trustworthy" (Titus 2:10, NLT).

When God gives you a friend like that, tested and true, cherish that friend. Never let him or her go.

> The friends thou hast, and their adoption tried,
> Grapple them to thy soul with hoops of steel.[2]

Doesn't Jesus love us with that absoluteness? The Bible says, "Having loved his own who were in the world, he loved them to the end" (John 13:1). And not because we deserve it. As soon as Peter denied Jesus that third time, the Lord turned and looked at him (Luke 22:61). Peter had proclaimed his own steadfast love: "I'll never deny you." All the disciples did (Matthew 26:35). And they all let him down. When Peter saw the Lord looking right into his face at that moment of utter betrayal, he finally saw himself. He knew that Jesus saw his failure and still loved him, and that friendship smote his heart. The King James Version says that our risen Lord is even now "touched with the feeling of our infirmities" (Hebrews 4:15). He does not despise us for our weakness. He is touched. That is how a friend feels. It's why we love John Newton's hymn:

> Could we bear from one another what He daily bears from us?
> Yet this glorious Friend and Brother loves us, though we treat Him thus.
> Though for good we render ill, He accounts us brethren still.

That is friendship. Total acceptance. Total forgiveness. A true friend knows who you really are and does not walk away. But there is more.

> Iron sharpens iron
>   and one man sharpens another. (Proverbs 27:17)

> Faithful are the wounds of a friend;
>   profuse are the kisses of an enemy. (Proverbs 27:6)

This is also part of a true friend—not only an all-accepting constancy but also a blunt honesty. Proverbs 24:26 says, "Whoever gives an honest answer kisses the lips." Real friendship is like sharpening the blade of a sword, the proverb says, because God wants every one of us to be sharp for him. By ourselves we become dull and blunted and lose our edge. Every one of us needs a friend who will not flatter us but will refine us. These proverbs are not meant to unleash reckless mouthing-off and self-appointed critics who think you really need their opinions. But these proverbs are about a true friend in your life who is making you better by respectful confrontation. The Bible says, "Let us consider how to stir up one another to love and good works" (Hebrews 10:24). A real friend will provoke you and challenge you. You will not agree with everything your friend says, but you will want to listen.

We all need that. Our various family backgrounds left every one of us at least a little weird. So we need an honest friend from outside the tightly knit family to round us out. Every one of us needs to go to another person and say, "Help me see myself. Help me get sharper for Christ." And if no other person in your church is good enough to play that role for you, the problem is you. If you do not know anyone well enough yet to trust them at that level, are you seeking that person out?

You must pursue this because, in one sense, you do not need a friend. Biologically you do not need a friend. Financially you can thrive without a friend. And as busy as we are these days, unless we are seeking Christ, friendship will end up at the bottom of the to-do list. But you cannot become wise without a Christian friend speaking into your life. It can be painful. But the wounds of an honest friend are faithful to help you grow.

There is something more here in these two proverbs. I wonder if you see it. When iron sharpens iron, it creates friction. When a friend wounds you, it hurts. So, do you see? There is a difference between hurting someone and harming someone. There is a difference between someone being loved and someone feeling loved. Jesus loved everyone well, and some people felt hurt. They were not harmed by him. They were loved by him. But they felt hurt. So they crucified him. If we don't understand this, then every time we feel hurt we will look for someone to blame and punish. We will make our emotional state someone else's fault. We might spread that version of events to other people in slander. But the truth is, a friend will inevitably hurt you with words that are respectful, true, and blunt. If you will receive it, you will grow in wisdom. The Beatles were right: "I get by with a little help from my friends."

How Can Friendship Go Wrong?

Whoever covers an offense seeks love,
but he who repeats a matter separates close friends. (Proverbs 17:9)

We disappoint our friends. We don't want to, but we do. So there will always be offenses. The wise person covers them with forgiveness, the way God does: "Blessed is the one . . . whose sin is covered" (Psalm 32:1). Why doesn't God keep embarrassing us with our failures? Because he wants our friendship. He covers our sins through Christ. It's what we do too, because we want our sinning friend more than we want payback. That is the mind of Christ.

Gossips do not understand that. Gossips do repeat a matter—not that they dredge it up over and over again. The word translated "repeats" means to mention the offense a second time. Just one repeat. So that person who sinned against you—did he admit it and ask your forgiveness? Then drop it. Don't mention it even one more time. You have regained a close friend! See the word "close"? A gossip can destroy a friendship that is close and has taken years to build through hard times. But now the gossip, the nag, the finger-pointer intensifies the offense to the point of alienation. God wants us to think carefully about what we say. It doesn't matter if what we feel like saying is factually true. Is it helpful? Is it creating a better future? What matters is the impact our words will have. We are constantly creating the conditions we will be stuck with five minutes from now. So how do we create the future we want? We keep remembering that all our sins have been forgiven by God and forgotten by him forever. He is creating those new conditions where we sinners can *live* again. Okay. Now we know how to treat each other.

> Whoever belittles his neighbor lacks sense,
>   but a man of understanding remains silent. (Proverbs 11:12)

The scenario here is one person in a power position, someone who is in the right, looking down on someone else, making him feel small. But a wise man knows that it is not enough to be right. Even if we are right, God wants us to humble ourselves with restraint. Don't answer every insult. Silence can preserve a friendship, a partnership, a marriage, a church.

> Let your foot be seldom in your neighbor's house,
>   lest he have his fill of you and hate you. (Proverbs 25:17)

Friends need time together, and friends need time *not* together. As Kenny Rogers sang, "You gotta know when to hold 'em and know when to fold 'em." In Heaven there will be a gazillion people, every one of them will like you, and they will never get tired of you. But until we are there, we are all weak enough that it is wise to ask ourselves when enough is enough. Benjamin Franklin said, "Guests, like fish, stink after three days." My dad understood that. Whenever he came to us for a visit, it always seemed too short. When he left, we wanted more. It added eagerness to our friendship.

> A brother offended is more unyielding than a strong city,
>   and quarreling is like the bars of a castle. (Proverbs 18:19)

The beginning of strife is like letting out water,
    so quit before the quarrel breaks out. (Proverbs 17:14)

Drive out a scoffer, and strife will go out,
    and quarreling and abuse will cease. (Proverbs 22:10)

It is so hard to stop a fight once it starts. No one ends up happy and satis-fied. Everyone feels injured and misunderstood. And then what do we do? Typically, we retreat into the castles of our minds: "Quarreling is like the bars of a castle." We bolt the door so tightly, only God can get through. How do we avoid going into that dark and lonely place? When the Christians in Corinth were suing each other, Paul got right to the point: "Why not rather suffer wrong? Why not rather be defrauded?" (1 Corinthians 6:7). If we are willing to lose the argument, we might win the friend.

Sadly, sometimes this doesn't work. Some people are impossible. For some people, facts don't matter, truth doesn't matter, fairness doesn't matter, finding a win-win doesn't matter. They are unsatisfiable. What then? "Drive out a scoffer." That makes a church safe for sinners who do want to grow and change.

But who is a "scoffer"? The Bible says, "Scoffer is the name of the arrogant, haughty man who acts with arrogant pride" (Proverbs 21:24). A scoffer is above everybody else—or so he thinks. He will not listen and fit in. So, what can you do when the scoffer is too superior to recognize common ground? Drive him out   and everyone else will breathe a sigh of relief. This is what elders are responsible to do in a church. The Bible says to church elders, "As for a person who stirs up division, after warning him once and then twice, have nothing more to do with him" (Titus 3:10). There comes a definite point when the troublemaker is shown the door. And if the elders chicken out, they then share in the sin and the destruction.

How Can Friendship Be Revived?

Do not say, "I will repay evil";
    wait for the LORD, and he will deliver you. (Proverbs 20:22)

Whoever conceals his transgressions will not prosper,
    but he who confesses and forsakes them will obtain mercy. (Proverbs 28:13)

If your enemy is hungry, give him bread to eat,
    and if he is thirsty, give him water to drink,
for you will heap burning coals on his head,
    and the LORD will reward you. (Proverbs 25:21, 22)

God has brought some of us into the study of the book of Proverbs just for this. There is so much injury today, so much sin, so much brokenness. Here is what God wants you to know: The best revenge is love. Whoever is mad at you—if you will relieve the pangs of his hunger, you will increase the pangs of his conscience. You might bring him to repentance. You might save his very soul. Isn't that reward enough? Paul quotes this proverb in Romans 12:20. He makes the point clear: "Do not be overcome by evil, but overcome evil with good" (Romans 12:21). Your hateful enemy expects you to be hateful in return. It's how the whole world works. But love will surprise that person the way Jesus keeps on surprising us. We treat him poorly, but he keeps on treating us like royalty, and it melts our hearts. Maybe you've seen the 1951 sci-fi movie *The Thing from Another World*. One of the members of an Arctic research team betrays all his comrades and nearly gets them killed. But when the report is filed by radio back to headquarters, the man speaking tells the story as if the offender had been the hero. All the other team members standing around, listening in, are saying, "Way to go."[3]

When Christ calls in his report on your life, he does not mention a single one of your betrayals. He absorbed them all into himself at the cross. What he says about you is his own heroism. He gives it to you freely. He loves us, his enemies, to make us his friends. If your former friend, now your enemy, can be won back, the love of Christ is the only way. His love is the only power in the universe that can change a human heart.

Who Is Our Truest Friend Always?

A man of many companions may come to ruin,
　　but there is a friend who sticks closer than a brother. (Proverbs 18:24)

Greater love has no one than this, that someone lay down his life for his friends. (John 15:13)

You might have many pseudo-friends who will let you down, even when everything is on the line. But you can also have one Super-Friend who sticks closer than a brother. When the Apostle Paul was put on trial before Caesar, all his friends hightailed it. But it was okay with Paul. He was not even angry. Why? "The Lord stood by me and strengthened me" (2 Timothy 4:17). Proverbs 18:24 is saying, real friends are not found in quantity but in quality. And no one offers us higher quality friendship than Jesus Christ.

When he laid down his life for his friends at the cross, he was forsaken, though he was loyal, so that we would never be forsaken, though we are disloyal. He was the offended brother, but he opened the castle of his heart. We put our feet frequently in his house, but he never wishes we would go away.

C. S. Lewis, in his essay on friendship, says that a new friendship starts out like this: "What? You too? I thought I was the only one."[4] Friends do not need to be alike. They just discover how much they have in common. Guess what you have in common with Christ? *Everything you care about the most.* He cares about you. He cares about your sin. He cares about your future. He thinks about you. He understands you. He loves you. You are not alone. He is here. You can receive him now.

Will you let the eternal friendship begin for you today?

20

Money

The blessing of the LORD makes rich,
and he adds no sorrow with it.

10:22

WISDOM IS SKILL FOR LIVING WELL IN THE SIGHT OF GOD AND MAN. We need wisdom every day, because the right thing to do is not always obvious. Solomon prayed for wisdom. He asked God for "an understanding mind . . . that I may discern between good and evil" (1 Kings 3:9). Why pray for that? Solomon had the Ten Commandments to help him discern between good and evil. But he needed more, and so do we. We all need "an understanding mind"—literally in the Hebrew, "a listening mind." Then we can discern between good and evil as we are making decisions moment by moment in the complexities of everyday life. So let's offer our Lord our listening minds as he coaches us with his wisdom about money.

But I wonder if there may be some awkwardness in raising the subject of money. Maybe you already know what I am going to say. You know I am going to tell you to tithe. And I should, because you should. Jesus said to the Pharisees, "You are careful to tithe even the tiniest income from your herb gardens, but you ignore the more important aspects of the law—justice, mercy and faith. You should tithe, yes, but do not neglect the more important things" (Matthew 23:23, NLT). The Pharisees tithed carefully from all their income, even the herbs from their backyard gardens, and Jesus did not tell them they were taking it too far. But he told them to pay attention to the

173

weightier matters of the Law as well. So let's not think of tithing as heroic, high-level commitment. Tithing is entry-level obedience, and then we go from there. Are you tithing?

What is tithing? A tithe is the first item in a Christian's monthly budget, the first check we write, 10 percent of our gross income. And that first check goes to the cause of Christ. How could it be otherwise? *Something* comes first in our budgets. Do we really want to say to our Lord, "I'll fit you in, if I can"? So we write out our personal budgets at home, on a legal pad or on a computer, and we put the Lord *first* with our tithe every month. This is basic obedience. It is simple. We just do the math.

Wisdom takes us further. Wisdom makes us sacrificial, like Christ. That kind of obedience is more than dutifully mathematical; it is beautiful and powerful and freeing. It opens us up to pursue the weightier matters of the Law with wholehearted devotion. But let's all admit that, sadly, money has an almost hypnotic spell over us. Money makes us feel secure and in control and important. Our itch for more money holds us back from bolder obedience. But tithing alone will not set us free. We should tithe. We also need God's wisdom to escape the illusions of money and live in the generosity of Christ. Let's receive that precious wisdom from him right now, as he reveals it in the book of Proverbs. Here are the three things he wants to say to us.

God Made Money a Blessing—and It's Available

> The blessing of the LORD makes rich,
>   and he adds no sorrow with it. (Proverbs 10:22)

Like it or not, the basic attitude of Proverbs toward money is positive: "The blessing of the LORD makes rich." If you have a money problem, the answer is not money. The answer is the Lord. Your employer does not provide for you; God does. If the blessing of the Lord makes rich, then our business is with *him*. As John Calvin wrote, "The Christian must surely be so disposed and minded that he feels within himself it is with God he has to deal throughout his life."[1] As the sage wrote, "The eyes of the LORD are in every place" (Proverbs 15:3). Our business is always with God first, and he is the best business partner in the universe. "He adds no sorrow." When you make money by the blessing of the Lord, you do not have to bend the rules, you can keep your promises, you do not have to overwork yourself, your conscience can stay clear, and you make enough money to share with others, which is joyful. There is no sorrow in that.

Why is the book of Proverbs basically positive about money? Because of the book of Genesis: "And God saw everything that he had made, and behold, it was very good" (Genesis 1:31). God has packed into this world vast potentialities for wealth creation. The wheat fields of the American Midwest, the breadbasket of the world—God made that. The gold and silver and gems hidden in the earth—God made all that. According to Genesis 2, God put gold, fine gold, in the world before sin ever came along (vv. 11, 12). And interestingly, it also says the gold was not evenly distributed all around but was located in one place, the land of Havilah. So God created a world in which some people would have more financial opportunity than others. Why? So they could share with others and become more like God himself, the ultimate Sharer.

The Biblical worldview is uniquely positive about the creation. Before the Bible was written, people in the ancient Near East saw the universe as the result of a battle between the good gods and the bad gods, making the world the leftovers of a cosmic catastrophe. The Greeks saw the universe as an icky material barrier to spirituality. But the Bible was written to protest every worldview that tarnishes the Creator and the creation. Our problem as human beings is not God. Our problem is not his creation. Our problem is that we look at God's creation in all its splendor and we think, "Oh, so this is how I can stop feeling empty—I'll make money." We bring our sadness to the creation and we say to it, "You are my happiness." That idolatry is what adds sorrow to our lives. The Bible says, "Some people, craving money, have . . . pierced themselves with many sorrows" (1 Timothy 6:10, NLT).

But the gospel gives us new eyes for seeing everything. Now we look out at that same creation and think, "If this is what God made, what better wealth must be in *him*?" Savonarola, the Italian reformer, put it this way: "What must not he possess who possesses the Possessor of all things?"[2] If the Creator is yours, your emptiness has found its fullness, however much money you have or however little money you have. The Bible says, "All things are yours" (1 Corinthians 3:21). God made everything for you. Why? To draw your heart up to him. We are swimming every moment in an ocean of divine generosity. God is not holding out. He is blessing us in every way that will not add sorrow to our lives.

But *how* does God bless us? How does God actually put his money into our pockets? Through the dignity of our own hard work.

A slack hand causes poverty,
    but the hand of the diligent makes rich. (Proverbs 10:4)

Poverty because of injustice is no disgrace, but laziness is. God made us for good, hard work. Our bodies thrive when they work. Our emotions are satisfied when we strive toward a goal and reach it. And when we have something to share with others as well, it really makes us happy. That is true wealth.

We are rediscovering in these times of economic recession that poverty is never far away. The diligent understand that. Things never turn out well automatically, even in good times. So "the hand of the diligent" intervenes, to keep making progress. The prosperity we Americans were born into is not a natural state of affairs. How did it happen? The Greatest Generation, after winning World War II, came home and built this country up by their diligent hands. The privileges we have inherited are the blessing of the Lord through "the hand of the diligent." And now it is our turn. God blesses through our hard work. If you are not going anywhere financially because you have not disciplined yourself and worked hard and made good use of your time and brains, you need to repent. God has not run out of blessing.

> Whoever works his land will have plenty of bread,
>> but he who follows worthless pursuits lacks sense. (Proverbs 12:11)

"He who follows worthless pursuits" can also be translated "a person who chases fantasies" (NLT). Is your career dream realistic? Is it productive? "Whoever works his land will have plenty of bread." God made us men especially to build something up and make it successful and use it not for self-glory but for the glory of God and the benefit of others. That takes humility as we plow one furrow one day and then turn around and plow the next furrow the next day, back and forth, doggedly, ruggedly, faithfully. How will the world be a better place because of what you do this week? What "land" are you developing in practical ways that work? Each week is a *God*-given tract of land, so to speak, and he is inviting us to make something of it.

> Wealth gained hastily will dwindle,
>> but whoever gathers little by little will increase it. (Proverbs 13:11)

Here is how God *doesn't* provide—the lottery and all get-rich-quick schemes. But how *does* God get us ahead? "Little by little." That is, by our patient, intelligent efforts over a lifetime—not by windfalls, but by handfuls.[3]

Why does God bless us "little by little"? Because he is building *us*. He is building in us the *character* that will not dwindle. For God, it's not about the money. I doubt that God feels one particle of emotion about American dollars. But he feels surging emotions about us. Little by little God is increasing us and preparing us to live forever and never dwindle. That is the backstory to all our financial ups and downs—the love of God for you and me.

I believe that God gives each of us exactly what he knows we need, and at the right time. Personally, I doubt that I will ever be rich. I probably could not be trusted with great wealth. Some people can be. Some of the sweetest Christians I have known are wealthy Christians—meek, kindhearted, generous. They handle money well. They do good with it. But for the rest of us, who will never be wealthy, here is God's wisdom for us:

> Better is a little with the fear of the LORD
>   than great treasure and trouble with it.
> Better is a dinner of herbs where love is
>   than a fattened ox and hatred with it. (Proverbs 15:16, 17)

"Better" is the word that restores our natural envy and restlessness to a wiser, calmer perspective. It is foolish to look at someone else's privileged life and think, "That is better than what I have." It is wise to consider what my own life would be without God's watchful care and think, "This is better than what I would have had." What if I did become rich but without the blessing of the Lord? Great treasure often brings trouble with it. But "godliness with contentment . . . is great gain" (1 Timothy 6:6).

We Make Money a Curse—and It's Powerful

In itself money is good, as a part of God's creation. But in our hands it can become destructive. The book of Proverbs alerts us to four dark powers that our hearts generate about money. These dark powers are control, conflict, confusion, and corruption.

> The people curse him who holds back grain,
>   but a blessing is on the head of him who sells it. (Proverbs 11:26)

This is about *control*. Someone selfishly hoards grain, to drive up the price. Grain was no luxury in the ancient world. It was basic to their diet. So holding back grain was a way to manipulate people at their point of real and daily need. Bruce Waltke articulates one of the central insights of the book of Proverbs this way: "The righteous are willing to disadvantage themselves to advantage the community; the wicked are willing to disadvantage the community to advantage themselves."[4] Isn't that why we put blessing on the head of our Lord Jesus? He disadvantaged himself to advantage us by his selfless life and death. He does not drive up the price. His love isn't even for sale. He gives it freely.

> A greedy man stirs up strife,
>> but the one who trusts in the LORD will be enriched. (Proverbs 28:25)

This is about *conflict*. The phrase translated "greedy" is literally "wide of appetite," that is, an inner drivenness that overlooks boundaries and warning signs and limits. A greedy person is unsatisfied with what he has. So he foolishly overreaches and triggers conflict with others. The Bible says, "You covet and cannot obtain, so you fight and quarrel" (James 4:2). Jesus did not come to take. He came to give, because he trusted in the Lord to be his Giver. And now he is being enriched with billions of people who gladly leave strife behind and unite together for him. This wisdom succeeds.

> The wicked earns deceptive wages,
>> but one who sows righteousness gets a sure reward. (Proverbs 11:18)

This is about *confusion*. The words for "deceptive wages" can also be translated "wages that are a lie." Selfishness tells us, "Get what you want. Then you'll be happy." Such "wisdom" may seem so obvious as to be unquestionable. But it is a lie, to confuse us. Jesus said, "Truly, truly, I say to you, unless a grain of wheat falls into the earth and dies, it remains alone; but if it dies, it bears much fruit" (John 12:24). His true wisdom is counterintuitive; but it gets a sure reward, as the emphatic "truly, truly" attests.

> Unequal weights are an abomination to the LORD,
>> and false scales are not good. (Proverbs 20:23)

This is about *corruption*. "Unequal weights" are any kind of dishonesty, any kind of cheating or cutting corners or false advertising. That is an "*abomination*" to the Lord. Strong language. An abomination in the Old Testament included sexual sin, for example (Leviticus 18:22). But here the Bible says that dishonest business practices are an "abomination." They are moral corruption. You might be sexually pure, but if you cheat people for money, your life is still an abomination in the sight of God. Do you owe anyone money you are not repaying? Do you have the relationship with God you think you have? The Bible says, "If you are a thief, quit stealing. Instead, use your hands for good hard work, and then give generously to others in need" (Ephesians 4:28, NLT). And where does glad-hearted generosity come from? The gospel.

Christ Saves Tightfisted Sinners—and He's Gracious

> One gives freely, yet grows all the richer;
>> another withholds what he should give, and only suffers want.

Whoever brings blessing will be enriched,
    and one who waters will himself be watered. (Proverbs 11:24, 25)

Reality surprises us. The reality is, selfish people end up poor in every sense. And openhanded people get richer and richer in all the ways that count. If you do not believe that enough that it redirects your money, look at Jesus. The Hebrew word translated "one gives freely" can be more literally rendered "one who scatters," like scattering seed, throwing it around freely and widely without paying attention to where every little seed might fall. The risen Lord Jesus has scattered the seed of the gospel on millions and millions of people, including you. He gives himself freely. And he is growing rich with your love back to him. His generosity is the secret to life, it is wisdom, and it is succeeding. Selfishness is poverty. Generosity is wealth.

Two things I ask of you;
    deny them not to me before I die:
Remove far from me falsehood and lying;
    give me neither poverty nor riches;
    feed me with the food that is needful for me,
lest I be full and deny you
    and say, "Who is the LORD?"
or lest I be poor and steal
    and profane the name of my God. (Proverbs 30:7–9)

This is the only prayer in the entire book of Proverbs. It may seem surprising. I mean, how is this for a life goal? Never to go broke, nor to get rich—because both are dangerous with temptation—but to live month-to-month in constant dependence on God and to do as much good with our money as we can. It might seem crazy, but that really is wisdom. My grandparents lived that way. Grandpa made decent money. But when they died in 1974, there was little left. They had given most of it away to missionaries and others. The family did not resent them. We were proud of them. What a great legacy!

But the best incentive for wise use of our money takes us to the New Testament and the fuller display of the glory of Jesus:

For you know the grace of our Lord Jesus Christ, that though he was rich, yet for your sake he became poor, so that you by his poverty might become rich. (2 Corinthians 8:9)

When Paul wrote this, he was raising money for the poor. How does he motivate for generosity? He does not appeal to our emotions with sob stories. He does not order our wills with commands. He shows us Jesus. Our Savior was rich with Heaven. But he gave it up and came down into our poverty, so that we might become rich with him forever. He lost, so that we could gain. That is his wisdom, it is true wisdom, and it works. Jesus was raised by the Father with a name above every name.

Now we know how life actually succeeds here in God's universe. Christ is our new wisdom. He changes what we do with our money.

21

Life and Death

PROVERBS 12:28

In the path of righteousness is life.

12:28

LIFE AND DEATH ARE A MAJOR THEME IN THE BOOK OF PROVERBS. The words "life" and "live" occur around fifty-six times in this book, and the words "death" and "die" around twenty times. And for us, when we say that something is "a matter of life and death," we mean that it matters above all else. We never forget the birth of a child. We never forget the funeral of a friend.

But life is more than having a pulse, and death is more than not having a pulse. The book of Proverbs gives us depth perception. Wisdom sees death as not just the physical event of a moment; wisdom sees death as a whole realm, a domain of human existence, in conflict with life. Think of it this way. You have a birthday. You know that day. It is on the calendar. You also have a death day. You do not know that day. But it too is on the calendar. You have an appointment out in the future. And beyond that moment of death, further on, the Old Testament sees the realm of death called Sheol. According to the book of Proverbs, death is both an event and a state beyond that event.

Still more, death casts a shadow over on this side, on us today. Death is encroaching on life right now in the forms of sickness, aging, suffering, fear, guilt, anxiety, confusion, boredom, and above all, sin. Any weakening of our vitality is death even now. Real life is more than a beating heart; real life is the vitality only God can give. And he does give it, gladly and freely, through the finished work of Christ on the cross. We receive it as we press the gospel into our hearts by faith. The risen Christ said, "Fear not. I am . . . the living one" (Revelation 1:17, 18).

We sinners stray into the territory of death every day. But in the book of Proverbs God is counseling us, alerting us to where death lurks. When the sage warns his son against sexual sin, for example, he says, "The dead are there" (Proverbs 9:18). There is a hell before Hell. But there is also a heaven before Heaven. Jesus said, "I came that they may have life and have it abundantly" (John 10:10). Jesus said, "Because I live, you also will live" (John 14:19).

This is what God wants for every one of us today: to die less and live more through Christ. He alone can set our consciences free from regret and dread and all forms of heart-death. Christ spreads new life to sinners, and on terms of grace. Life *pours* out of him. Let's open up to him right now. We do that by believing his Word more than we believe anything else. "You never know how much you really believe anything until its truth or falsehood becomes a matter of life and death to you."[1]

How Christ Moves Us Further into Life

In the path of righteousness is life,
and in its pathway there is no death. (Proverbs 12:28)

There is a way that seems right to a man,
but its end is the way to death. (Proverbs 14:12; 16:25)

Treasures gained by wickedness do not profit,
but righteousness delivers from death. (Proverbs 10:2)

Whoever keeps the commandment keeps his life;
he who despises his ways will die. (Proverbs 19:16)

The wage of the righteous leads to life,
the gain of the wicked to sin. (Proverbs 10:16)

The key metaphor here is "path," "way," and "end." There is a road, and there is a destination. The question is, where are we going with our lives? Everyone is on a journey. We can choose our own path, but we cannot choose our own consequences, our own destination. "In the path of righteousness [only] is *life*."

Two questions here are obvious. One, what is righteousness? Two, is this righteousness legalism? The proverb says, "The wage of the righteous leads to life." Is that a legalistic pay-as-you-go plan?

But first, what is righteousness? In Deuteronomy Moses tells us about the weights people used in the marketplace to measure the goods they were selling. He says, "A full and fair weight you shall have" (Deuteronomy 25:15). If the weight says 16 ounces, it is 16 ounces. No one is cheating. The weight is full and fair, because it's true to what 16 ounces really are as an objective reality. And the word translated "fair" is our word "righteous." A righteous weight represents the true standard, the reality. Even so, a righteous person sees a standard outside himself, he sees *outside* himself what a human being should be, and he acknowledges that the standard is Christ. A righteous person bows down before Christ and says, "I want to be true not to myself but to you."

We modern people should have no problem, therefore, with external standards. We do not mind grooming an image. We want to look cool. The standard of coolness controls how we dress, and more. We are adjusting to a standard. So is it really unacceptable to see a moral order outside ourselves? The gospel says that Christ is the standard to which we should adjust. Not an abstract ethical ideal, but a person. Christ is the true human being. Recently, on The Gospel Coalition website, Dr. Tim Keller blogged about a new book profiling the beliefs of young adults from around eighteen to twenty-three. The author of the book relates how he asked people "if their moral convictions (some of which were very strong) were mainly subjective feelings or really true to reality. He found that most had difficulty even understanding what he was asking." We are being taught in our world today to see ourselves as our own moral authority moving through a series of life episodes and making decisions on the fly in terms of personal cost-benefit.[2] We are being taught that there is no moral order out there to take into account. But according to the book of Proverbs, that pathway leads into more and more death. How can a marriage be stable that way? How can you trust your mate, or anyone for that matter? Do you even know who *you* really are or who you are going to be an hour from now? Righteousness is becoming truer to Christ, because in his path is *life*.

Two, is this legalism? No. Legalism is obeying God with a wrong motive—to earn points on his scorecard. The book of Proverbs is not teaching us that false "righteousness." It is not saying that a high-quality life is something we *earn* by obeying God. The gospel is clear. We are "not under law but under grace" (Romans 6:14). Then it follows up with the obvious question: "Are we to sin because we are not under law but under grace?" (Romans 6:15). In other words, does rejecting legalism and coming under grace make sin no big deal anymore? Does grace make obedience non-urgent? Paul's answer there in Romans 6 is practical, like the reasoning here in the book of Proverbs: "When you were slaves of sin, you were free from the control of righteousness. And what gain did that bring you? Things that now make you ashamed, for their end is death. But now . . . you have gains that lead to holiness, and the end is eternal life" (Romans 6:20–22, REB).

Here is the insight. We *will* give ourselves to *something*. We just will: "When you were *slaves* of sin . . . " Let's never think that the further we move from God, the more freedom we gain. When we hear that whisper in our hearts saying, "You want to be free. So be careful. Don't give too much of yourself to God"—the instant that thought creeps in, we must stop and ask ourselves, "Where did that come from? What is the hidden motive *behind* that thought? Hey, Thought, where did you come from? If I follow your path, where will you take me—into more life or into more death?" There are many paths to choose from, but there is no possibility of no consequences. The only question is, do we want to stay slaves of sin? The law of God cannot get us off that deadly path, but the grace of God will not leave us there.

If you have had your bellyful of sin and you feel wounded and it seems like nobody cares anymore and your heart is broken because you are experiencing the bitter aftertaste of death, Jesus Christ does *not* say to you, "I told you so." He says, "Come to me, and I will give you rest." There is nothing degrading or shaming in Christ. If we will come to him, he accepts us as we are, he loves us into obedience, and we find by experience that obeying him really is the path of life.

Frank Laubach was a missionary to the Philippines. He created a way of teaching literacy that helped about 60,000,000 people around the world learn to read. He is the only missionary to be honored with a U.S. postage stamp. In 1984 our Postal Service put out a 30¢ stamp with Frank Laubach's picture on it. He helped a lot of people.

But more deeply, Frank Laubach longed for God. So one year he tried an experiment. He spent 1930 on a daily journey going deeper with God. He was a busy man. But he wanted to live his busy life with God. Here is what he wrote to a friend on January 26, 1930:

> Do not try this, unless you feel dissatisfied with your own relationship with God, but at least allow me to realize all the leadership of God I can. I am disgusted with the pettiness and futility of my unled self. If the way out is not more perfect slavery to God, then what is the way out?[3]

Too often we are not enslaved to God. We are enslaved to ourselves in our pettiness and futility. Deep inside us is not one whole integrated self but rather a committee of competing selves. There they are, sitting around a board room inside our heads—the work self, the married self, the parent self, the secret self, the dating self, whatever. Our different selves sit around this big table, each one shouting out its demands and staking its claims and fearful of being overlooked. When the committee votes, it is rarely unanimous.

If you are divided and frustrated like that, if you are not wholehearted for Christ, you are dying more than you have to. Today can be a turning point for you. Admit to yourself who you really are. Turn to Christ, the Friend of sinners. Become honest with him, moment by moment: "Blessed is the man against whom the Lord counts no iniquity, *and in whose spirit there is no deceit*" (Psalm 32:2). If you are out of control, admit it to him, and he will help you, he will guide you into his path, he will bring you under his control. Give yourself to him, and he will give you more and more of the life you long for.

How the Life of Christ Spreads to More People

> The fear of the LORD is a fountain of life,
>   that one may turn away from the snares of death. (Proverbs 14:27)

> The teaching of the wise is a fountain of life,
>   that one may turn away from the snares of death. (Proverbs 13:14)

"The fear of the LORD" is internal, private, personal. "The teaching of the wise" is external, public, shared. We need *both* to satisfy our thirst at the overflowing, ever-fresh, reviving "fountain of life." How does that actually work? A tender heart toward Christ and a gospel-centered church—both together keep us refreshed and safe from the snares—we might say, the land mines—of death.

Let's keep our eyes peeled for two dangers. One is our own hearts saying, "I've heard all this before." Theologically aware people can become arrogant and not even notice it. Let's always remember that life is not in theology; life is in Christ. He is not a concept. He is a living person. If we will treat him that way, he will keep us from the snare of theological pride, which is death. Let's also be careful to keep our churches in hyper-focus on the gospel—good news for bad people through the finished work of Christ on the cross. There is only one fountain of life (singular), and there are many snares of death (plural). The fountain is Christ. And he *flows out* whenever humility and wise teaching converge. That is revival, and we want it for everyone in our world today.

> A gentle tongue is a tree of life,
>   but perverseness in it breaks the spirit. (Proverbs 15:4)

The fruit of the righteous is a tree of life,
    and whoever captures souls is wise. (Proverbs 11:30)

Did you know there is a way for people in our broken world to reexperi-
ence the tree of life from the Garden of Eden? It can happen through, of all
things, words: "A gentle tongue [word] is a tree of life." What is the sage
talking about? You can see in the margin of the ESV that "a gentle tongue"
can also be translated "a healing tongue." Perverse words are powerful. They
break a person's spirit. But wise words are more powerful. They soothe and
heal. And the most powerfully healing words are gospel words: "Take heart,
my son; your sins are forgiven" (Matthew 9:2), "There is therefore now no
condemnation for those who are in Christ Jesus" (Romans 8:1), "I will never
leave you nor forsake you" (Hebrews 13:5), and many more. These are the
divine words that heal the perverse words that have broken our spirits. And
these are the words Christ wants more people to hear through us. It is not our
mission merely to tell people how sinful they are but how life-giving Christ
is. That is healing.

And it works. The "fruit" of the righteous in Proverbs 11:30 is their
influence. God wired us to find righteousness attractive. True righteousness
is humane and beautiful. We move toward it and find ourselves captivated.
And Christ spreads the influence of his tree of life through us. You and I, as
believers, are his strategy. Again, it is not our mission to prove people wrong
but to win them to Christ. He cares so deeply for everyone we know. And
as we join him in caring, his influence enters in. When the gospel goes out
of our mouths, the power of God is going out, creating new life in everyone
who listens with an open heart.

What Is Your Next Step with Christ?

My son, eat honey, for it is good,
    and the drippings of the honeycomb are sweet to your taste.
Know that wisdom is such to your soul;
    if you find it, there will be a future,
    and your hope will not be cut off. (Proverbs 24:13, 14)

I find this delightful. The sage is saying that pleasure awakens us to how
good wisdom is. So maybe this is what you should do today. Bake some
cornbread, take it hot out of the oven, cut out a big piece, open it up, put on a
dab of real butter, watch it melt over the steaming cornbread, take the plastic
honey bear and squeeze honey all over that cornbread, then put a forkful in
your mouth, followed up with a big drink of cold milk. As you savor that
delight, "know that wisdom is such to your soul."

Your soul has senses too. And God's wisdom is sweet to your deepest self. You enjoy it by *eating* it. You cannot enjoy his wisdom just by looking at it. But if you will take it and chew on it and swallow it—well, as we all know, eating and joy go together. So it is with Christ. And the pleasures he gives do not wear out. They are your future, the proverb says, and your hope cannot be cut off. In fact, enjoying Christ personally is your *only* future. Look what happens if we refuse:

> He who is often reproved, yet stiffens his neck,
>   will suddenly be broken beyond healing. (Proverbs 29:1)

When God rebukes us, he is only calling us away from death back into life and pleasure in Christ. He is patient. But if we stubbornly refuse and refuse and refuse, then every heartbeat is more rebellion against a God of love, and his patience will end. His patience ended toward a whole culture at Sodom and Gomorrah. His patience can end at any time toward individuals and churches. Isn't God pleading with every one of us right now? We are in a moment of mercy right now—if we will bow low enough to receive it. Will we? Will we obey the promptings of the Spirit and step out in new obedience beginning today, however God is speaking to each of us? He is ready right now to do a new work in you and me. If we are not believing and eager, what are we thinking? That God is *obligated* to wait until we feel good and ready? How can we assume that tomorrow God will still be holding the door open for us? If we do not take advantage of this opportunity right now, why should he give us more? He has already waited. *This is our moment with the Lord Jesus Christ*, who gives us every gracious incentive to humble ourselves and become decisive for him:

> Fear not, for I am . . . the living one. I died, and behold I am alive forev-
> ermore, and I have the keys of Death and Hades. (Revelation 1:17, 18)

> I am the way, and the truth, and the life. (John 14:6)

He did not say, "There is a way." He said, "I am the way." Will you follow him? Will you take your Spirit-prompted next step into new obedience to Christ? He welcomes you. New life awaits you. Right now.

Soli Deo gloria!

Notes

Chapter One: Why the Book of Proverbs Matters

1. Derek Kidner, *The Proverbs: An Introduction and Commentary* (Downers Grove, IL: InterVarsity Press, 1964), p. 13.

2. Jonathan Edwards, *Works*, Vol. I (Edinburgh: The Banner of Truth Trust, 1979 reprint), p. 397.

3. Frederick William Faber, "Workman of God O Lose Not Heart," in *The Church Hymnary: Revised Edition* (London: Oxford University Press, 1927), #520.

4. C. S. Lewis, *The Pilgrim's Regress* (Grand Rapids: Eerdmans, 1973 reprint), p. 125.

5. Bruce K. Waltke, *The Book of Proverbs: Chapters 1–15* (Grand Rapids: Eerdmans, 2004), pp. 58–63.

6. Quoted in J. S. Brooker, ed., *T. S. Eliot: The Contemporary Reviews* (Cambridge: Cambridge University Press, 2004), p. 310.

7. John Pollock, *Billy Graham: The Authorized Biography* (New York: McGraw-Hill, 1966), p. 248.

8. Nicholas Carr, "Is Google Making Us Stupid?," *The Atlantic*, July/August 2008. Accessed via Google, http://www.theatlantic.com/magazine/archive/2008/07/is-google-making-us-stupid/6868/, March 12, 2010.

9. Michael V. Fox, *Proverbs 1–9* (New Haven, CT: Yale University Press, 2006), p. 43: "Indeed, according to the Prologue, the *peti* is the primary audience of Proverbs' instruction."

10. John A. Kitchen, *Proverbs* (Fearn, UK: Mentor, 2006), p. 731.

11. Martyn Lloyd-Jones, *Seeking the Face of God: Nine Reflections on the Psalms* (Wheaton: Crossway Books, 2005), p. 34.

12. DeVern Fromke, quoted in Ray Ortlund, *Let the Church Be the Church* (Nashville: Word, 1983), p. 43.

Chapter Two: Let's Begin

1. I thank Dr. Bruce Waltke for putting the matter this way in a sermon preached at Believer's Chapel, Dallas, Texas.

2. Miriam Lichtheim, *Ancient Egyptian Literature, A Book of Readings: Volume II, The New Kingdom* (Berkeley: University of California Press, 1976), pp. 146–163.

3. George M. Marsden, *Jonathan Edwards: A Life* (New Haven, CT: Yale University Press, 2003), p. 77.

4. The ESV concludes verse 5 with a comma, so that verse 6 continues the thought. But I see verse 5 as parenthetical, with verse 6 resuming the purpose statements of verses 2–4. Therefore, I conclude verse 5 with a dash, matching the dash at the end of verse 4.

5. These three sub-categories of wisdom come from E. J. Schnabel, "Wisdom," in *New Dictionary of Biblical Theology*, ed. T. Desmond Alexander and Brian S. Rosner (Leicester, UK: Inter-Varsity Press, 2000), p. 843.

6. C. J. Mahaney, *Humility: True Greatness* (Sisters, OR: Multnomah, 2005), p. 13.

7. Michael V. Fox, *Proverbs 1–9* (New Haven, CT: Yale University Press, 2006), p. 40.

8. See Henri Blocher, "The Fear of the Lord as the 'Principle' of Wisdom," *Tyndale Bulletin* 28 (1977): 3–28.

9. C. S. Lewis, *Mere Christianity* (New York: Macmillan, 1958), p. 96.

10. Rene Descartes, *Discourse on Method* (New York: The Liberal Arts Press, 1950), p. 21.

11. See Gerhard von Rad, *Wisdom in Israel* (Nashville: Abingdon Press, 1972), p. 67.

12. Iris Murdoch, *Metaphysics as a Guide to Morals* (New York: Penguin, 1993), p. 54.

13. C. S. Lewis, *The Lion, the Witch and the Wardrobe* ((New York: Collier Books, 1972), pp. 75, 76.

14. Kenneth Grahame, *The Wind in the Willows* (New York: Charles Scribner's Sons, 1916), pp. 180–182. Italics his.

Chapter Three: Violence!

1. Eric Clapton, *Clapton: The Autobiography* (New York: Broadway Books, 2007), p. 150: "I instinctively understood that the success of the record [*461 Ocean Boulevard*] depended entirely on the kind of chemistry we [in the band] developed."

2. On the foregoing, see Cornelius Plantinga Jr., *Not The Way It's Supposed to Be: A Breviary of Sin* (Grand Rapids: Eerdmans, 1995), pp. 113–128; C. S. Lewis, *A Preface to Paradise Lost* (London: Oxford University Press, 1979), p. 95.

3. Bruce K. Waltke and M. O'Connor, *Introduction to Biblical Hebrew Syntax* (Winona Lake, IN : Eisenbrauns, 1990), 5.4a.

4. Paul Johnson, *A History of the Modern World from 1917 to the 1980s* (London: Weidenfeld and Nicolson, 1983), p. 729: "By the 1980s, state action [in the course of the twentieth century] had been responsible for the violent or unnatural deaths of over 100 million people, more perhaps than it had hitherto succeeded in destroying during the whole of human history up to 1900."

5. Paul Johnson, *Intellectuals* (New York: Harper & Row, 1988), p. 337:

> Now here we come to the great crux of the intellectual life: the attitude to violence. It is the fence at which most secular intellectuals, be they pacifist or not, stumble and fall into inconsistency—or, indeed, into sheer incoherence. They may renounce it in theory, as indeed in logic they must since it is the antithesis of rational methods of solving problems. But in practice they find themselves from time to time endorsing it—what might be called the Necessary Murder Syndrome—or approving its use by those with whom they sympathize.

6. Quoted in Herbert Schlossberg, *Idols for Destruction* (Nashville: Thomas Nelson, 1983), p. 52.

7. C. H. Spurgeon, *The Treasury of the New Testament*, Vol. 1 (Grand Rapids: Zondervan, 1950), p. 175.

Chapter Four: A Storm Is Coming

1. A. W. Tozer, *The Counselor* (Camp Hill, PA: Christian Publications, 1993), p. 116.

2. Available online: http://www.lyricsreg.com/lyrics/regina+spektor/LAUGHING+WITH/.

3. Cynthia Heimel, *If You Can't Live without Me, Why Aren't You Dead Yet?* (New York: Grove Press, 1991), pp. 13, 14. I thank Dr. Tim Keller for drawing my attention to this statement.

4. C. S. Lewis, *The Great Divorce* (New York: Macmillan, 1973), p. 72. Italics his.

5. Ted Wise, "Pornography," sermon preached at Peninsula Bible Church, June 11, 1972, Discovery Papers #491, pp. 4, 5.

Chapter Five: How We Can Grow

1. C. S. Lewis, *The Weight of Glory* (New York: HarperCollins, 2001), p. 190.

2. "The Gospel According to Oprah," on The Mockingbird Blog, February 9, 2009; http://www.mbird.com/2009/02/gospel-according-to-oprah/.

3. See C. S. Lewis, "The Inner Ring," in *The Weight of Glory* (New York: HarperCollins, 2001), pp. 141–157.

Chapter Six: The Wisdom That *Helps* Us

1. Quoted in Donald G. Bloesch, *A Theology of Word and Spirit* (Downers Grove, IL: InterVarsity Press, 1992), p. 127.

2. C. S. Lewis, *The Problem of Pain* (New York: Macmillan, 1972), p. 115.

3. Mark Rutherford, *The Revolution in Tanner's Lane* (New York: Jonathan Cape and Harrison Smith, 1929), p. 266.

4. A. W. Tozer, *The Root of the Righteous* (Harrisburg, PA: Christian Publications, 1955), p. 50.

5. Bruce K. Waltke, *The Book of Proverbs: Chapters 1–15* (Grand Rapids: Eerdmans, 2004), pp. 237, 244, renders this, "in all your ways desire his presence," a valid paraphrase.

6. Quoted in Iain H. Murray, *Wesley and Men Who Followed* (Edinburgh: The Banner of Truth, 2003), p. 87.

Chapter Seven: Wisdom at the Extremes of Life

1. Bruce K. Waltke and M. O'Connor, *Introduction to Biblical Hebrew Syntax* (Winona Lake, IN : Eisenbrauns, 1990), 24.2f-h.

2. Geerhardus Vos, "The Doctrine of the Covenant in Reformed Theology," *Redemptive History and Biblical Interpretation* (Phillipsburg, NJ: Presbyterian and Reformed, 1980), pp. 234–267.

3. David Wells, *God in the Wasteland: The Reality of Truth in a World of Fading Dreams* (Grand Rapids: Eerdmans, 1994), pp. 88–117.

4. Os Guinness, *The Gravedigger File: Papers on the Subversion of the Modern Church* (Downers Grove, IL: InterVarsity Press, 1983), pp. 49–70.

5. Ibid., p. 63.

6. *Matthew Henry's Commentary on the Whole Bible*, Vol. III (McLean, VA: MacDonald Publishing, n.d.), p. 804. Style updated.

7. C. S. Lewis, *The Problem of Pain* (New York: Macmillan, 1972), pp. 42, 43.

Chapter Eight: Why Wisdom Matters, What Wisdom Creates

1. John Calvin, *Institutes*, 2.2.15.

2. Bruce K. Waltke, *The Book of Proverbs: Chapters 1–15* (Grand Rapids: Eerdmans, 2004), p. 257.

3. John Piper, "The Great Work of God: Rain," http://www.desiringgod.org/resource-library/taste-see-articles/the-great-work-of-god-rain.

4. C. S. Lewis, *The Weight of Glory and Other Addresses* (Grand Rapids: Eerdmans, 1974), pp. 13, 14. Italics his.

5. John E. Smith, Harry S. Stout, and Kenneth P. Minkema, eds., *A Jonathan Edwards Reader* (New Haven, CT: Yale University Press, 1995), p. 245.

6. So in NEB, REB; Waltke, *Proverbs 1–15*, pp. 253, 265.

Chapter Nine: The Only Path into Life

1. Gardiner Spring, "God the Greatest Giver," in *Pulpit Ministrations, or Sabbath Readings*, Vol. II (New York: Harper and Brothers, 1864), p. 211.

2. Available at http://www.monergism.com/Chalmers%2C%20Thomas%20-%20The%20Exlpulsive%20Power%20of%20a%20New%20Af.pdf.

3. Proverbs 1:8, 10, 15; 2:1; 3:1, 11, 21.

4. G. K. Chesterton, "The Ethics of Elfland," in *Orthodoxy* (Garden City, NJ: Doubleday, 1959), pp. 46–65.

5. *St. Athanasius on the Incarnation*, with an Introduction by C. S. Lewis (London: A. R. Mowbray, 1979), pp. 4, 5.

6. Eugene Van Ness Goetchius, *The Language of the New Testament* (New York: Scribner's, 1965), p. xi; see James Boswell, *The Life of Samuel Johnson*, Vol. IV (London: John Murray, 1831), p. 355.

7. John Milton, *Paradise Lost* (London: Tonson and Draper, 1750), I:261.

8. Geneen Roth, *Women, Food and God* (New York: Scribner, 2010), p. 32. Italics original.

9. Alexander Pope, "Essay on Man," in *The Poetical Works of Alexander Pope* (London: Macmillan, 1907), p. 206.

10. The ESV reads, "Put away from you crooked speech, and put devious talk far from you." But a more literal translation reveals the sage's deliberate references to anatomy.

Chapter Ten: Bitter Honey and Sweet Water

1. Chapter title from David A. Hubbard, *The Communicator's Commentary: Proverbs* (Dallas: Word Books, 1989), p. 88.

2. This is available at http://theresurgence.com/search/results?q=Porn-Again+Christian.

3. Martyn Lloyd-Jones, *Revival* (Wheaton: Crossway Books, 1987), p. 300.

4. *The Poetical Works of Lord Byron*, Vol. II (London: John Murray, 1879), p. 415.

5. The ESV reads, "Let your fountain be blessed." That is not a wrong translation. But some readers might misunderstand it as permission, which is not the point. "May your fountain be blessed," an equally valid translation, is more clearly understandable as a prayer, which is the point.

6. Bruce K. Waltke, *The Book of Proverbs: Chapters 1–15* (Grand Rapids: Eerdmans, 2004), p. 321.

7. Leland Ryken, *Worldly Saints: The Puritans as They Really Were* (Grand Rapids: Zondervan, 1986), p. 39.

8. Alister E. McGrath, *Christian Spirituality: An Introduction* (Oxford, UK: Blackwell, 1999), pp. 158, 159.

Chapter Eleven: Responsibility, Opportunity, Unity

1. The ESV text reads "hasten," while the ESV margin reads, and I believe more accurately, "humble yourself." Michael V. Fox, *Proverbs 1–9* (New Haven, CT: Yale University Press, 2006), pp. 210, 213 goes so far as to render it "grovel."

2. See http://www.ftc.gov/bcp/edu/pubs/consumer/credit/cre06.shtm. Accessed July 9, 2010.

3. Fox, *Proverbs 1–9*, pp. 210, 213; NEB, REB.

4. Verse 10 is probably the sage's quotation of the sluggard, as in the NASB. The contrast is between the "little" compromises of verse 10 and the forceful consequences of verse 11. The sluggard deceives himself with such thoughts.

5. In both lines of verse 11, I preserve the possessive pronoun "your" in the Hebrew text. The sluggard has squandered his existence. He has only himself to blame.

6. I acknowledge my debt here to Derek Kidner, *The Proverbs: An Introduction and Commentary* (Downers Grove, IL: InterVarsity Press, 1964), pp. 42, 43.

7. I acknowledge my debt here to Haddon Robinson, "Proverbial Pests," *Christianity Today*, April 27, 1992, pp. 26–28.

8. Ray Ortlund, *Lord, Make My Life a Miracle* (Ventura, CA: Regal Books, 1974), p. 151.

Chapter Twelve: Why Our Sexuality Matters to God

1. Henry Chadwick, trans., *Saint Augustine: Confessions* (Oxford: The University Press, 1991), p. 5.

2. Bruce K. Waltke, preaching at Believer's Chapel, Dallas, Texas.

3. See news.bbc.co.uk/2/hi/2319863.stm. Accessed July 13, 2010.

4. William Arnot, *Laws from Heaven for Life on Earth: Illustrations of the Book of Proverbs* (London: T. Nelson and Sons, 1884), p. 311.

5. David Atkinson, *The Message of Proverbs: Wisdom for Life* (Downers Grove, IL: InterVarsity Press, 1996), p. 77.

6. Piotr Bienkowski and Alan Millard, eds., *British Museum Dictionary of the Ancient Near East* (London: British Museum Press, 2000), p. 156.

7. William M. Struthers, *Wired for Intimacy* (Downers Grove, IL: InterVarsity Press, 2010).

Chapter Thirteen: The Worldview of Wisdom

1. ESV marginal reading.

2. T. S. Eliot, "The Hollow Men," in *12 Poets*, Glenn Leggett, ed. (Chicago: Holt, Rinehart and Winston, 1958), p. 284.

3. Thomas C. Oden, *Two Worlds: Notes on the Death of Modernity in America & Russia* (Downers Grove, IL: InterVarsity Press, 1992), pp. 93–107.

4. I thank Dr. Bruce Waltke for bringing this to my attention through a sermon preached at Believer's Chapel, Dallas, Texas.

5. Alexander Heidel, *The Gilgamesh Epic and Old Testament Parallels* (Chicago: University of Chicago Press, 1958), p. 236.

6. C. S. Lewis, *Mere Christianity* (New York: HarperCollins, 2001), p. 134: "Aim at Heaven, and you will get earth 'thrown in'; aim at earth, and you will get neither."

7. Bruce K. Waltke, *The Book of Proverbs: Chapters 1–15* (Grand Rapids: Eerdmans, 2004), pp. 417–422, argues that the sense is not "like a master workman" but "constantly." The parallelism favors his interpretation:

then I was constantly beside him,
and I was daily his delight,
rejoicing before him always.

8. The ESV marginal translation seems preferable, since the emphasis of verses 30, 31 is the joy of Wisdom in the creation, not the Creator's joy in Wisdom.

9. William J. Bouwsma, *John Calvin: A Sixteenth Century Portrait* (Oxford: Oxford University Press, 1988), pp. 134, 135.

10. *The Sabbath Recorder*, Vol. 78, No. 1 (January 4, 1915), p. 157.

11. Gerhard von Rad, *Old Testament Theology*, Vol. I (New York: Harper and Row, 1962), p. 449.

Chapter Fourteen: It's Decision Time

1. William Romaine, *Treatises on the Life, Walk and Triumph of Faith* (Glasgow: William Collins, 1830), p. 305. Style updated.

2. Paul Joüon, *A Grammar of Biblical Hebrew* (Rome: Pontifical Biblical Institute, 1991), § 88Mk.

3. The ESV marginal translation is more literal and more accurate.

4. Nigel M. de S. Cameron and Sinclair B. Ferguson, eds., *Pulpit & People: Essays in Honour of William Still on His 75th Birthday* (Edinburgh: Rutherford House, 1986), p. 48.

5. Dietrich Bonhoeffer, *The Cost of Discipleship* (New York: Macmillan, 1959), p. 35.

6. William McKane, *Proverbs: A New Approach* (Philadelphia: Westminster Press, 1970), p. 399.

7. Quoted in Skye Jethani, "Is the Church Abetting a Generation of Sarcasm?" http://www.huffingtonpost.com/skye-jethani/is-the-church-abetting-a_b_579124.html, May 18, 2010. Accessed May 23, 2011.

8. Henry Chadwick, trans., *Saint Augustine: Confessions* (Oxford: Oxford University Press, 1991), p. 29.

9. C. H. Spurgeon, "None but Jesus," http://www.spurgeon.org/sermons/0361.htm. Accessed December 30, 2010.

10. Walter Hooper, ed., *The Collected Letters of C. S. Lewis*, Vol. III (San Francisco: HarperCollins, 2007), p. 152.

Chapter Fifteen: The Tongue

1. Derek Kidner, *The Proverbs: An Introduction and Commentary* (Downers Grove, IL: InterVarsity Press, 1964), p. 46.

2. Bruce K. Waltke, "Fundamentals for Preaching the Book of Proverbs, Part 1," *Bibliotheca Sacra* 165 (2008): 4.

3. I thank Derek Kidner for his subject studies, on pp. 31–56 of his commentary, *The Proverbs,* which provided the pattern of my topical studies.

4. Allen P. Ross, "Proverbs," in Frank E. Gaebelein, ed., *The Expositor's Bible Commentary*, Vol. V (Grand Rapids: Zondervan, 1991), pp. 897–903.

5. Edmond G. Addeo and Robert E. Burger, *EgoSpeak: Why No One Listens to You* (Radnor, PA: Chilton Book Company, 1973), p. 201.

6. Francis A. Schaeffer, *The Mark of the Christian* (Downers Grove, IL: Inter-Varsity Press, 1970), pp. 21, 22.

7. Dietrich Bonhoeffer, *Life Together* (New York: Harper & Row, 1954), p. 23.

Chapter Sixteen: Humility

1. C. J. Mahaney, *Humility: True Greatness* (Sisters: Multnomah, 2005), p. 15.

2. See www.nytimes.com/2002/02/03/magazine/the-trouble-with-self-esteem. html, February 23, 2002; accessed June 2, 2011.

3. Bob Dylan, "The Times They Are A-changin'" (1964).

4. Cordelia Fine, *A Mind of Its Own: How Your Brain Distorts and Deceives* (New York: W. W. Norton, 2006), p. 2.

5. Jonathan Edwards, *Works*, Vol. I (Edinburgh: Banner of Truth Trust, 1979), pp. 399, 400. Style updated.

6. C. S. Lewis, *Mere Christianity* (New York: Macmillan, 1958), p. 94.

Chapter Seventeen: Family

1. A. W. Tozer, *The Knowledge of the Holy* (New York: Harper & Row, 1961), p. 11.

2. Francis A. Schaeffer, *The Church at the End of the 20ᵗʰ Century* (Downers Grove, IL: InterVarsity Press, 1970), pp. 81, 82.

3. Michael V. Fox, *Proverbs 1–9* (New Haven, CT: Yale University Press, 2006), p. 40.

4. Patricia Cohen, "Long Road to Adulthood Is Growing Even Longer," http://www.nytimes.com/2010/06/13/us/13generations.html?scp=1&sq=%22Long%20Road%20to%20Adulthood%20Is%20Growing%20Even%20Longer%22&st=cse, June 13, 2010.

5. I wish I could acknowledge where I found this sequence of accomplishments by the young, but I cannot remember the source. My apologies.

Chapter Eighteen: Emotions

1. I take much of the following from B. B. Warfield, "The Emotional Life of Our Lord," in *The Person and Work of Christ* (Grand Rapids: Baker, 1970), pp. 93–145.

2. See A. B. Bruce, *The Humiliation of Christ* (Edinburgh: T. & T. Clark, 1905), p. 334.

3. Charles Bridges, *A Commentary on Proverbs* (Edinburgh: Banner of Truth Trust, 1987), p. 250.

4. Miroslav Volf, *Exclusion and Embrace: A Theological Exploration of Identity, Otherness and Reconciliation* (Nashville: Abingdon Press, 1996), p. 302.

5. Joseph Epstein, *Envy: The Seven Deadly Sins* (Oxford: The University Press, 2003), dust jacket notes.

6. J. R. R. Tolkien, *The Fellowship of the Ring* (Boston: Houghton Mifflin, 1994), p. 58.

Chapter Nineteen: Friendship

1. Daniel David Luckenbill, ed., *Ancient Records of Assyria and Babylonia*, Vol. I (Chicago: The University of Chicago Press, 1926), p. 110.

2. Shakespeare, *Hamlet*, Act 1, Scene 3, Lines 62, 63.

3. Paul F. M. Zahl, *Grace in Practice: A Theology of Everyday Life* (Grand Rapids: Eerdmans, 2007), p. 210.

4. C. S. Lewis, *The Four Loves* (New York: Harcourt Brace Jovanovich, 1960), p. 96.

Chapter Twenty: Money

1. John Calvin, *Institutes*, 3.7.2.

2. James Hastings, *The Great Texts of the Bible: Job to Psalm XXIII* (New York: Charles Scribner's Son, 1913), p. 267.

3. See Bruce K. Waltke, *The Book of Proverbs: Chapters 1–15* (Grand Rapids: Eerdmans, 2004), p. 561.

4. Ibid., p. 97.

Chapter Twenty-one: Life and Death

1. C. S. Lewis, *A Grief Observed* (New York: Seabury Press, 1961), p. 21.

2. See   thegospelcoalition.org/blogs/tgc/2010/10/06/late-modern-or-postmodern. Accessed October 9, 2010.

3. Frank C. Laubach, *Letters by a Modern Mystic* (Westwood, NJ: Fleming H. Revell, 1958), pp. 11, 12.

Scripture Index

General Index

Index of Sermon Illustrations

211

Sexual Ethics
The murder of quarterback Steve McNair reminds us that sexual integrity is a matter of life and death, 90
Inevitable consequences of sexual sin illustrated in man's phoning for a call girl, and it's his daughter, causing him to have an apparent heart attack, 108
Ancient Babylonian goddess Ishtar was the goddess of both love and war, a reminder that sexual sin and violence go together, 111

Sin
Martyn Lloyd-Jones: we won't see our own sin unless we have a knowledge of God, 22
Sailmaker hippie: it is impossible to sin and not suffer because of it, but that suffering corrects us, 48
Frank Sinatra song "My Way" is the opposite of a life of faith, 65–66
John Wesley: a hundred preachers who fear nothing but sin and desire nothing but God would establish God's kingdom on earth, 66
Thomas Chalmers in sermon "The Expulsive Power of a New Affection": we will change only when we see that Christ will make us alive in ways our sins cannot, 82
Satan, in John Milton's *Paradise Lost*, when he fell: "Evil, be thou my good," 86
Alexander Pope: "familiar with [vice's] face, we first endure, then pity, then embrace," 87
Martyn Lloyd-Jones: giving in to sin too long or too often can lead to an inability or an unwillingness to repent, 91
Lord Byron, on the cost of sin: "The worm, the canker, and the grief are mine alone," 92
The fallenness of creation is described in T. S. Eliot's description of modern culture as "shape without form, shade without color, paralyzed force, gesture without motion," 114

Spurgeon: Jesus Christ came into the world to save sinners, 130
C. S. Lewis: "You write much about your own sins. Beware . . . lest humility should pass over into anxiety or sadness," 130
Lauren Slater in "The Trouble with Self-esteem": criminals "are racist or violent because they don't feel bad enough about themselves," 142
Bob Kauflin: "My sin is that my heart is pleased or troubled as things please or trouble me, without my having a regard to Christ," 143
Like King Lear, we feel more sinned against than sinning, 145

Slander
Los Angeles woman's suicide note: "They said," 134
Vince Foster's suicide note: "Here [Washington] ruining people is considered sport," 134

Sovereignty of God
God even uses evil for his purposes, as seen in Gandalf's comment about Gollum: "My heart tells me that he has some part to play yet, for good or ill, before the end," 163

Spiritual Revolution
Francis Schaeffer: we must teach our young people not to be conservatives (maintaining the status quo) but revolutionaries, 154

Spiritual Riches
Savonarola: "What must not he possess who possesses the Possessor of all things?" 175

Suffering
Regina Spektor song: suffering makes us more serious about God, 47
Sailmaker hippie: it is impossible to sin and not suffer because of it, but that suffering corrects us, 48

William Cowper hymn: "Behind a frowning providence He hides a smiling face," 71

C. S. Lewis in *The Problem of Pain*: "it is natural for us to wish that God had designed for us a less glorious and less arduous destiny; but then we are wishing not for more love but for less," 71

Unbelief
Unbelief puts off receiving God's offer, 44

Vice
Alexander Pope: "familiar with [vice's] face, we first endure, then pity, then embrace," 87

Violence
Violence comes from the "My neighborhood!" attitude portrayed in *The Godfather Part 2*, 79

Ancient Babylonian goddess Ishtar was the goddess of both love and war, a reminder that sexual sin and violence go together, 111

Virtue
Jonathan Edwards: true virtue consists of union of heart with God, 76

Wisdom
C. S. Lewis's *Pilgrim's Regress* reminds us that the path of wisdom leads us through a valley of humiliation, 18

T. S. Eliot asks, "Where is the wisdom we have lost in knowledge?" 20

What ABC's are to reading Shakespeare, what playing the scales are to performing Bach, what 2 + 2 = 4 is to doing calculus, the fear of the Lord is to wisdom, 32

Jesus' wisdom is dangerous like fire, 45

John Piper: the wisdom of God in creation is seen in the marvels of simple rainfall, 75-76

Galadriel, the elf queen in The Lord of the Rings, is a picture of Lady Wisdom in the book of Proverbs, 114

God's wisdom should be as much a delight to us as warm cornbread with lots of butter and honey, 186

The Word of God
Dietrich Bonhoeffer sees speaking the Word of God to one another as one way of loving one another, 136

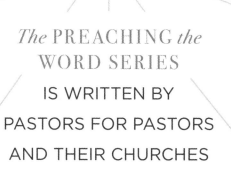

The PREACHING *the* WORD SERIES

IS WRITTEN BY

PASTORS FOR PASTORS

AND THEIR CHURCHES

crossway.org/preachingtheword